Lyrics of the Hearthside

AMS PRESS
NEW YORK

Paul Laurence Dunbar.

Lyrics of the Hearthside

By

Paul Laurence Dunbar

New York
Dodd, Mead and Company
1899

Library of Congress Cataloging in Publication Data

Dunbar, Paul Laurence, 1872-1906.
  Lyrics of the hearthside.

  I. Title.
PS1556.L7 1972   811'.4   70-164802
ISBN 0-404-00037-1

1/8/52

Reprinted from the edition of 1899, New York
First AMS edition published in 1972
Manufactured in the United States of America

International Standard Book Number: 0-404-00037-1

AMS PRESS INC.
NEW YORK, N.Y.   10003

TO ALICE

CONTENTS.

———◆———

Contents.

Contents.

Contents.

Lyrics of the Hearthside.

LOVE'S APOTHEOSIS.

LOVE me. I care not what the circling years
      To me may do.
If, but in spite of time and tears,
      You prove but true.

Love me — albeit grief shall dim mine eyes,
      And tears bedew,
I shall not e'en complain, for then my skies
      Shall still be blue.

Love me, and though the winter snow shall pile,
      And leave me chill,
Thy passion's warmth shall make for me, mean-
    while,
      A sun-kissed hill.

Lyrics of the Hearthside.

And when the days have lengthened into years,
    And I grow old,
Oh, spite of pains and griefs and cares and
    fears,
      Grow thou not cold.

Then hand and hand we shall pass up the hill,
    I say not down ;
That twain go up, of love, who 've loved their
    fill, —
      To gain love's crown.

Love me, and let my life take up thine own,
    As sun the dew.
Come, sit, my queen, for in my heart a throne
    Awaits for you !

THE PARADOX.

I AM the mother of sorrows,
  I am the ender of grief;
I am the bud and the blossom,
  I am the late-falling leaf.

I am thy priest and thy poet,
  I am thy serf and thy king;
I cure the tears of the heartsick,
  When I come near they shall sing.

White are my hands as the snow-drop;
  Swart are my fingers as clay;
Dark is my frown as the midnight,
  Fair is my brow as the day.

Battle and war are my minions,
  Doing my will as divine;
I am the calmer of passions,
  Peace is a nursling of mine.

Lyrics of the Hearthside.

Speak to me gently or curse me,
  Seek me or fly from my sight;
I am thy fool in the morning,
  Thou art my slave in the night.

Down to the grave will I take thee,
  Out from the noise of the strife;
Then shalt thou see me and know me —
  Death, then, no longer, but life.

Then shalt thou sing at my coming,
  Kiss me with passionate breath,
Clasp me and smile to have thought me
  Aught save the foeman of Death.

Come to me, brother, when weary,
  Come when thy lonely heart swells;
I 'll guide thy footsteps and lead thee
  Down where the Dream Woman dwells.

OVER THE HILLS.

OVER the hills and the valleys of dreaming
    Slowly I take my way.
Life is the night with its dream-visions teeming,
    Death is the waking at day.

Down thro' the dales and the bowers of loving,
    Singing, I roam afar.
Daytime or night-time, I constantly roving, —
    Dearest one, thou art my star.

WITH THE LARK.

NIGHT is for sorrow and dawn is for joy,
　　Chasing the troubles that fret and annoy;
Darkness for sighing and daylight for song, —
Cheery and chaste the strain, heartfelt and
　　strong.
All the night through, though I moan in the
　　dark,
I wake in the morning to sing with the lark.

Deep in the midnight the rain whips the leaves,
Softly and sadly the wood-spirit grieves.
But when the first hue of dawn tints the sky,
I shall shake out my wings like the birds and
　　be dry;
And though, like the rain-drops, I grieved
　　through the dark,
I shall wake in the morning to sing with the
　　lark.

With the Lark.

On the high hills of heaven, some morning to
  be,
Where the rain shall not grieve thro' the leaves
  of the tree,
There my heart will be glad for the pain I have
  known,
For my hand will be clasped in the hand of
  mine own ;
And though life has been hard and death's path-
  way been dark,
I shall wake in the morning to sing with the
  lark.

IN SUMMER.

OH, summer has clothed the earth
    In a cloak from the loom of the sun !
And a mantle, too, of the skies' soft blue,
    And a belt where the rivers run.

And now for the kiss of the wind,
    And the touch of the air's soft hands,
With the rest from strife and the heat of life,
    With the freedom of lakes and lands.

I envy the farmer's boy
    Who sings as he follows the plow ;
While the shining green of the young blades lean
    To the breezes that cool his brow.

He sings to the dewy morn,
    No thought of another's ear ;
But the song he sings is a chant for kings
    And the whole wide world to hear.

8

In Summer.

He sings of the joys of life,
   Of the pleasures of work and rest,
From an o'erfull heart, without aim or art ;
   'T is a song of the merriest.

O ye who toil in the town,
   And ye who moil in the mart,
Hear the artless song, and your faith made strong
   Shall renew your joy of heart.

Oh, poor were the worth of the world
   If never a song were heard, —
If the sting of grief had no relief,
   And never a heart were stirred.

So, long as the streams run down,
   And as long as the robins trill,
Let us taunt old Care with a merry air,
   And sing in the face of ill.

THE MYSTIC SEA.

THE smell of the sea in my nostrils,
    The sound of the sea in mine ears ;
The touch of the spray on my burning face,
    Like the mist of reluctant tears.

The blue of the sky above me,
    The green of the waves beneath ;
The sun flashing down on a gray-white sail
    Like a scimitar from its sheath.

And ever the breaking billows,
    And ever the rocks' disdain ;
And ever a thrill in mine inmost heart
    That my reason cannot explain.

So I say to my heart, " Be silent,
    The mystery of time is here ;
Death's way will be plain when we fathom the
        main,
    And the secret of life be clear."

A Sailor's Song.

A SAILOR'S SONG.

OH for the breath of the briny deep,
    And the tug of a bellying sail,
With the sea-gull's cry across the sky
And a passing boatman's hail.
For, be she fierce or be she gay,
The sea is a famous friend alway.

Ho! for the plains where the dolphins play,
And the bend of the mast and spars,
And a fight at night with the wild sea-sprite
When the foam has drowned the stars.
And, pray, what joy can the landsman feel
Like the rise and fall of a sliding keel?

Fair is the mead; the lawn is fair
And the birds sing sweet on the lea;
But the echo soft of a song aloft

Lyrics of the Hearthside.

Is the strain that pleases me ;
And swish of rope and ring of chain
Are music to men who sail the main.

Then, if you love me, let me sail
While a vessel dares the deep ;
For the ship 's my wife, and the breath of life
Are the raging gales that sweep ;
And when I 'm done with calm and blast,
A slide o'er the side, and rest at last.

The Bohemian.

THE BOHEMIAN.

BRING me the livery of no other man.
    I am my own to robe me at my pleasure.
  Accepted rules to me disclose no treasure:
What is the chief who shall my garments plan?
  No garb conventional but I 'll attack it.
  (Come, why not don my spangled jacket?)

ABSENCE.

GOOD-NIGHT, my love, for I have dreamed
    of thee
In waking dreams, until my soul is lost—
Is lost in passion's wide and shoreless sea,
Where, like a ship, unruddered, it is tost
Hither and thither at the wild waves' will.
There is no potent Master's voice to still
This newer, more tempestuous Galilee !

The stormy petrels of my fancy fly
In warning course across the darkening green,
And, like a frightened bird, my heart doth cry
And seek to find some rock of rest between
The threatening sky and the relentless wave.
It is not length of life that grief doth crave,
But only calm and peace in which to die.

14

Absence.

Here let me rest upon this single hope,
For oh, my wings are weary of the wind,
And with its stress no more may strive or cope.
One cry has dulled mine ears, mine eyes are
       blind, —
Would that o'er all the intervening space,
I might fly forth and see thee face to face.
I fly; I search, but, love, in gloom I grope.

Fly home, far bird, unto thy waiting nest;
Spread thy strong wings above the wind-swept
       sea.
Beat the grim breeze with thy unruffled breast
Until thou sittest wing to wing with me.
Then, let the past bring up its tales of wrong;
We shall chant low our sweet connubial song,
Till storm and doubt and past no more shall be!

HER THOUGHT AND HIS.

THE gray of the sea, and the gray of the sky,
  A glimpse of the moon like a half-
    closed eye.
The gleam on the waves and the light on the
  land,
A thrill in my heart, — and — my sweetheart's
  hand.

She turned from the sea with a woman's grace,
And the light fell soft on her upturned face,
And I thought of the flood-tide of infinite bliss
That would flow to my heart from a single kiss.

But my sweetheart was shy, so I dared not ask
For the boon, so bravely I wore the mask.
But into her face there came a flame : —
I wonder could she have been thinking the
  same?

16

THE RIGHT TO DIE.

I HAVE no fancy for that ancient cant
  That makes us masters of our destinies,
And not our lives, to hold or give them up
As will directs ; I cannot, will not think
That men, the subtle worms, who plot and plan
And scheme and calculate with such shrewd wit,
Are such great blund'ring fools as not to know
When they have lived enough.

                  Men court not death
When there are sweets still left in life to taste.
Nor will a brave man choose to live when he,
Full deeply drunk of life, has reached the dregs,
And knows that now but bitterness remains.
He is the coward who, outfaced in this,
Fears the false goblins of another life.
I honor him who being much harassed
Drinks of sweet courage until drunk of it, —
Then seizing Death, reluctant, by the hand,
Leaps with him, fearless, to eternal peace !

BEHIND THE ARRAS.

AS in some dim baronial hall restrained,
    A prisoner sits, engirt by secret doors
And waving tapestries that argue forth
Strange passages into the outer air;
So in this dimmer room which we call life,
Thus sits the soul and marks with eye intent
That mystic curtain o'er the portal death;
Still deeming that behind the arras lies
The lambent way that leads to lasting light.
Poor fooled and foolish soul!   Know now that
    death
Is but a blind, false door that nowhere leads,
And gives no hope of exit final, free.

When the Old Man Smokes.

WHEN THE OLD MAN SMOKES.

IN the forenoon's restful quiet,
　　When the boys are off at school,
When the window lights are shaded
　　And the chimney-corner cool,
Then the old man seeks his armchair,
　　Lights his pipe and settles back;
Falls a-dreaming as he draws it
　　Till the smoke-wreaths gather black.

And the teardrops come a-trickling
　　Down his cheeks, a silver flow—
Smoke or memories you wonder,
　　But you never ask him,—no;
For there 's something almost sacred
　　To the other family folks
In those moods of silent dreaming
　　When the old man smokes.

19

Lyrics of the Hearthside.

Ah, perhaps he sits there dreaming
　　Of the love of other days
And of how he used to lead her
　　Through the merry dance's maze ;
How he called her " little princess,"
　　And, to please her, used to twine
Tender wreaths to crown her tresses,
　　From the " matrimony vine."

Then before his mental vision
　　Comes, perhaps, a sadder day,
When they left his little princess
　　Sleeping with her fellow clay.
How his young heart throbbed, and pained
　　　him !
　　Why, the memory of it chokes !
Is it of these things he 's thinking
　　When the old man smokes?

But some brighter thoughts possess him,
　　For the tears are dried the while.
And the old, worn face is wrinkled
　　In a reminiscent smile,

When the Old Man Smokes.

From the middle of the forehead
  To the feebly trembling lip,
At some ancient prank remembered
  Or some long unheard-of quip.

Then the lips relax their tension
  And the pipe begins to slide,
Till in little clouds of ashes,
  It falls softly at his side ;
And his head bends low and lower
  Till his chin lies on his breast,
And he sits in peaceful slumber
  Like a little child at rest.

Dear old man, there 's something sad'ning,
  In these dreamy moods of yours,
Since the present proves so fleeting,
  All the past for you endures.
Weeping at forgotten sorrows,
  Smiling at forgotten jokes ;
Life epitomized in minutes,
  When the old man smokes.

Lyrics of the Hearthside.

THE GARRET.

WITHIN a London garret high,
　　Above the roofs and near the sky,
My ill-rewarding pen I ply
　　To win me bread.
This little chamber, six by four,
Is castle, study, den, and more, —
Altho' no carpet decks the floor,
　　Nor down, the bed.

My room is rather bleak and bare ;
I only have one broken chair,
But then, there 's plenty of fresh air, —
　　Some light, beside.
What tho' I cannot ask my friends
To share with me my odds and ends,
A liberty my aerie lends,
　　To most denied.

The Garret.

The bore who falters at the stair
No more shall be my curse and care,
And duns shall fail to find my lair
    With beastly bills.
When debts have grown and funds are short,
I find it rather pleasant sport
To live " above the common sort "
    With all their ills.

I write my rhymes and sing away,
And dawn may come or dusk or day:
Tho' fare be poor, my heart is gay,
    And full of glee.
Though chimney-pots be all my views;
'T is nearer for the winging Muse,
So I am sure she 'll not refuse
    To visit me.

Lyrics of the Hearthside.

TO E. H. K.

ON THE RECEIPT OF A FAMILIAR POEM.

TO me, like hauntings of a vagrant breath
　　From some far forest which I once have
　　　　known,
　The perfume of this flower of verse is blown.
Tho' seemingly soul-blossoms faint to death,
Naught that with joy she bears e'er withereth.
　　So, tho' the pregnant years have come and
　　　　flown,
　　Lives come and gone and altered like mine
　　　　own,
This poem comes to me a shibboleth :

Brings sound of past communings to my ear,
　　Turns round the tide of time and bears me
　　　　back
　　　Along an old and long untraversed way ;
Makes me forget this is a later year,
　　Makes me tread o'er a reminiscent track,
　　　Half sad, half glad, to one forgotten day !

24

A Bridal Measure.

A BRIDAL MEASURE.

COME, essay a sprightly measure,
    Tuned to some light song of pleasure.
  Maidens, let your brows be crowned
  As we foot this merry round.

From the ground a voice is singing,
From the sod a soul is springing.
  Who shall say 't is but a clod
  Quick'ning upward toward its God?

Who shall say it? Who may know it,
That the clod is not a poet
  Waiting but a gleam to waken
  In a spirit music-shaken?

Phyllis, Phyllis, why be waiting?
In the woods the birds are mating.
  From the tree beside the wall,
  Hear the am'rous robin call.

Lyrics of the Hearthside.

Listen to yon thrush's trilling;
Phyllis, Phyllis, are you willing,
　　When love speaks from cave and tree,
　　Only we should silent be?

When the year, itself renewing,
All the world with flowers is strewing,
　　Then through Youth's Arcadian land,
　　Love and song go hand in hand.

Come, unfold your vocal treasure,
Sing with me a nuptial measure, —
　　Let this springtime gambol be
　　Bridal dance for you and me.

VENGEANCE IS SWEET.

WHEN I was young I longed for Love,
    And held his glory far above
All other earthly things.   I cried :
" Come, Love, dear Love, with me abide ; "
And with my subtlest art I wooed,
And eagerly the wight pursued.
But Love was gay and Love was shy,
He laughed at me and passed me by.

Well, I grew old and I grew gray,
When Wealth came wending down my way.
I took his golden hand with glee,
And comrades from that day were we.
Then Love came back with doleful face,
And prayed that I would give him place.
But, though his eyes with tears were dim,
I turned my back and laughed at him.

Lyrics of the Hearthside.

A HYMN.

AFTER READING "LEAD, KINDLY LIGHT."

LEAD gently, Lord, and slow,
  For oh, my steps are weak,
And ever as I go,
  Some soothing sentence speak;

That I may turn my face
  Through doubt's obscurity
Toward thine abiding-place,
  E'en tho' I cannot see.

For lo, the way is dark;
  Through mist and cloud I grope,
Save for that fitful spark,
  The little flame of hope.

Lead gently, Lord, and slow,
  For fear that I may fall;
I know not where to go
  Unless I hear thy call.

A Hymn.

My fainting soul doth yearn
  For thy green hills afar;
So let thy mercy burn —
  My greater, guiding star!

JUST WHISTLE A BIT.

JUST whistle a bit, if the day be dark,
  And the sky be overcast:
If mute be the voice of the piping lark,
  Why, pipe your own small blast.

And it's wonderful how o'er the gray sky-track
The truant warbler comes stealing back.
But why need he come? for your soul's at rest,
And the song in the heart,— ah, that is best.

Just whistle a bit, if the night be drear
  And the stars refuse to shine:
And a gleam that mocks the starlight clear
  Within you glows benign.

Till the dearth of light in the glooming skies
Is lost to the sight of your soul-lit eyes.
What matters the absence of moon or star?
The light within is the best by far.

30

Just Whistle a Bit.

Just whistle a bit, if there 's work to do,
   With the mind or in the soil.
And your note will turn out a talisman true
   To exorcise grim Toil.

It will lighten your burden and make you feel
That there 's nothing like work as a sauce for a
      meal.
And with song in your heart and the meal in —
      its place,
There 'll be joy in your bosom and light in your
      face.

Just whistle a bit, if your heart be sore ;
   'T is a wonderful balm for pain.
Just pipe some old melody o'er and o'er
   Till it soothes like summer rain.

And perhaps 't would be best in a later day,
When Death comes stalking down the way,
To knock at your bosom and see if you 're fit,
Then, as you wait calmly, just whistle a bit.

THE BARRIER.

THE Midnight wooed the Morning-Star,
  And prayed her : " Love come nearer ;
Your swinging coldly there afar
  To me but makes you dearer ! "

The Morning-Star was pale with dole
  As said she, low replying :
" Oh, lover mine, soul of my soul,
  For you I too am sighing.

" But One ordained when we were born,
  In spite of Love's insistence,
That Night might only view the Morn
  Adoring at a distance."

But as she spoke the jealous Sun
  Across the heavens panted.
" Oh, whining fools," he cried, " have done ;
  Your wishes shall be granted ! "

The Barrier.

He hurled his flaming lances far;
  The twain stood unaffrighted —
And midnight and the Morning-Star
  Lay down in death united !

DREAMS.

DREAM on, for dreams are sweet:
  Do not awaken !
Dream on, and at thy feet
  Pomegranates shall be shaken.

Who likeneth the youth
  Of life to morning?
'T is like the night in truth,
  Rose-coloured dreams adorning.

The wind is soft above,
  The shadows umber.
(There is a dream called Love.)
  Take thou the fullest slumber !

In Lethe's soothing stream,
  Thy thirst thou slakest.
Sleep, sleep ; 't is sweet to dream.
  Oh, weep when thou awakest !

The Dreamer.

THE DREAMER.

TEMPLES he built and palaces of air,
    And, with the artist's parent-pride aglow,
His fancy saw his vague ideals grow
Into creations marvellously fair;
He set his foot upon Fame's nether stair.
    But ah, his dream, — it had entranced him so
    He could not move. He could no farther go;
But paused in joy that he was even there!

He did not wake until one day there gleamed
    Thro' his dark consciousness a light that
        racked
His being till he rose, alert to act.
But lo! what he had dreamed, the while he
        dreamed,
    Another, wedding action unto thought,
    Into the living, pulsing world had brought.

35

WAITING.

THE sun has slipped his tether
    And galloped down the west.
(Oh, it 's weary, weary waiting, love.)
The little bird is sleeping
    In the softness of its nest.
Night follows day, day follows dawn,
And so the time has come and gone :
    And it 's weary, weary waiting, love.

The cruel wind is rising
    With a whistle and a wail.
(And it 's weary, weary waiting, love.)
My eyes are seaward straining
    For the coming of a sail ;
But void the sea, and void the beach
Far and beyond where gaze can reach !
    And it 's weary, weary waiting, love.

Waiting.

I heard the bell-buoy ringing —
  How long ago it seems !
(Oh, it 's weary, weary waiting, love.)
And ever still, its knelling
  Crashes in upon my dreams.
The banns were read, my frock was sewn ;
Since then two seasons' winds have blown —
  And it 's weary, weary waiting, love.

The stretches of the ocean
  Are bare and bleak to-day.
(Oh, it 's weary, weary waiting, love.)
My eyes are growing dimmer —
  Is it tears, or age, or spray ?
But I will stay till you come home.
Strange ships come in across the foam !
  But it 's weary, weary waiting, love.

THE END OF THE CHAPTER.

AH, yes, the chapter ends to-day;
    We even lay the book away;
But oh, how sweet the moments sped
Before the final page was read!

We tried to read between the lines
The Author's deep-concealed designs;
But scant reward such search secures;
You saw my heart and I saw yours.

The Master, — He who penned the page
And bade us read it, — He is sage:
And what he orders, you and I
Can but obey, nor question why.

We read together and forgot
The world about us.   Time was not.
Unheeded and unfelt, it fled.
We read and hardly knew we read.

38

The End of the Chapter.

Until beneath a sadder sun,
We came to know the book was done.
Then, as our minds were but new lit,
It dawned upon us what was writ;

And we were startled.   In our eyes,
Looked forth the light of great surprise.
Then as a deep-toned tocsin tolls,
A voice spoke forth : " Behold your souls ! "

I do, I do.   I cannot look
Into your eyes : so close the book.
But brought it grief or brought it bliss,
No other page shall read like this !

SYMPATHY.

I KNOW what the caged bird feels, alas!
    When the sun is bright on the upland
        slopes;
When the wind stirs soft through the springing
        grass,
And the river flows like a stream of glass;
    When the first bird sings and the first bud
        opes,
And the faint perfume from its chalice steals —
I know what the caged bird feels!

I know why the caged bird beats his wing
    Till its blood is red on the cruel bars;
For he must fly back to his perch and cling
When he fain would be on the bough a-swing;
    And a pain still throbs in the old, old scars
And they pulse again with a keener sting —
I know why he beats his wing!

Sympathy.

I know why the caged bird sings, ah me,
   When his wing is bruised and his bosom
      sore, —
When he beats his bars and he would be free ;
It is not a carol of joy or glee,
   But a prayer that he sends from his heart's
      deep core,
But a plea, that upward to Heaven he flings —
I know why the caged bird sings !

LOVE AND GRIEF.

OUT of my heart, one treach'rous winter's
    day,
I locked young Love and threw the key away.
Grief, wandering widely, found the key,
And hastened with it, straightway, back to me,
With Love beside him.   He unlocked the door
And bad Love enter with him there and stay.
And so the twain abide for evermore.

LOVE'S CHASTENING.

Once Love grew bold and arrogant of air,
Proud of the youth that made him fresh and
    fair ;
So unto Grief he spake, " What right hast thou
To part or parcel of this heart ? "   Grief's brow
Was darkened with the storm of inward strife ;
Thrice smote he Love as only he might dare,
And Love, pride purged, was chastened all his
    life.

42

MORTALITY.

A SHES to ashes, dust unto dust,
　　What of his loving, what of his lust?
What of his passion, what of his pain?
What of his poverty, what of his pride?
Earth, the great mother, has called him again:
Deeply he sleeps, the world's verdict defied.
Shall he be tried again?　Shall he go free?
Who shall the court convene?　Where shall it be?
No answer on the land, none from the sea.
Only we know that as he did, we must:
You with your theories, you with your trust, —
Ashes to ashes, dust unto dust!

LOVE.

A LIFE was mine full of the close concern
  Of many-voiced affairs. The world sped
   fast;
 Behind me, ever rolled a pregnant past.
A present came equipped with lore to learn.
Art, science, letters, in their turn,
  Each one allured me with its treasures vast;
  And I staked all for wisdom, till at last
Thou cam'st and taught my soul anew to yearn.
 I had not dreamed that I could turn away
From all that men with brush and pen had
   wrought;
  But ever since that memorable day
When to my heart the truth of love was brought,
 I have been wholly yielded to its sway,
And had no room for any other thought.

44

She Gave Me a Rose.

SHE GAVE ME A ROSE.

SHE gave me a rose,
  And I kissed it and pressed it.
I love her, she knows,
  And my action confessed it.
She gave me a rose,
  And I kissed it and pressed it.

Ah, how my heart glows,
  Could I ever have guessed it?
It is fair to suppose
  That I might have repressed it:
She gave me a rose,
  And I kissed it and pressed it.

'T was a rhyme in life's prose
  That uplifted and blest it.
Man's nature, who knows
  Until love comes to test it?
She gave me a rose,
  And I kissed it and pressed it.

45

DREAM SONG. I.

L ONG years ago, within a distant clime,
  Ere Love had touched me with his wand
   sublime,
I dreamed of one to make my life's calm May
The panting passion of a summer's day.
And ever since, in almost sad suspense,
I have been waiting with a soul intense
To greet and take unto myself the beams,
Of her, my star, the lady of my dreams.

O Love, still longed and looked for, come to
  me,
Be thy far home by mountain, vale, or sea.
My yearning heart may never find its rest
Until thou liest rapt upon my breast.
The wind may bring its perfume from the south,
Is it so sweet as breath from my love's mouth?
Oh, naught that surely is, and naught that seems
May turn me from the lady of my dreams.

DREAM SONG. II.

PRAY, what can dreams avail
    To make love or to mar?
The child within the cradle rail
    Lies dreaming of the star.
But is the star by this beguiled
To leave its place and seek the child?

The poor plucked rose within its glass
    Still dreameth of the bee;
But, tho' the lagging moments pass,
    Her Love she may not see.
If dream of child and flower fail,
Why should a maiden's dreams prevail?

Lyrics of the Hearthside.

CHRISTMAS IN THE HEART.

THE snow lies deep upon the ground,
    And winter's brightness all around
Decks bravely out the forest sere,
With jewels of the brave old year.
The coasting crowd upon the hill
With some new spirit seems to thrill;
And all the temple bells achime
Ring out the glee of Christmas time.

In happy homes the brown oak-bough
Vies with the red-gemmed holly now;
And here and there, like pearls, there show
The berries of the mistletoe.
A sprig upon the chandelier
Says to the maidens, " Come not here ! "
Even the pauper of the earth
Some kindly gift has cheered to mirth !

Christmas in the Heart.

Within his chamber, dim and cold,
There sits a grasping miser old.
He has no thought save one of gain, —
To grind and gather and grasp and drain.
A peal of bells, a merry shout
Assail his ear: he gazes out
Upon a world to him all gray,
And snarls, "Why, this is Christmas Day!"

No, man of ice, — for shame, for shame!
For "Christmas Day" is no mere name.
No, not for you this ringing cheer,
This festal season of the year.
And not for you the chime of bells
From holy temple rolls and swells.
In day and deed he has no part—
Who holds not Christmas in his heart!

THE KING IS DEAD.

AYE, lay him in his grave, the old dead
    year !
His life is lived — fulfilled his destiny.
Have you for him no sad, regretful tear
To drop beside the cold, unfollowed bier?
Can you not pay the tribute of a sigh?

Was he not kind to you, this dead old year?
Did he not give enough of earthly store?
Enough of love, and laughter, and good cheer?
Have not the skies you scanned sometimes been
    clear?
How, then, of him who dies, could you ask
    more?

It is not well to hate him for the pain
He brought you, and the sorrows manifold.
To pardon him these hurts still I am fain;

The King is Dead.

For in the panting period of his reign,
He brought me new wounds, but he healed the
     old.

One little sigh for thee, my poor, dead friend —
One little sigh while my companions sing.
Thou art so soon forgotten in the end ;
We cry e'en as thy footsteps downward tend :
" The king is dead ! long live the king ! "

118152

THEOLOGY.

THERE is a heaven, for ever, day by day,
  The upward longing of my soul doth tell
    me so.
There is a hell, I'm quite as sure; for pray,
If there were not, where would my neigh-
    bours go?

Resignation.

RESIGNATION.

LONG had I grieved at what I deemed abuse ;
　　But now I am as grain within the mill.
If so be thou must crush me for thy use,
　　Grind on, O potent God, and do thy will !

LOVE'S HUMILITY.

AS some rapt gazer on the lowly earth,
    Looks up to radiant planets, ranging far,
So I, whose soul doth know thy wondrous worth
Look longing up to thee as to a star.

Precedent.

PRECEDENT.

THE poor man went to the rich man's doors,
    " I come as Lazarus came," he said.
The rich man turned with humble head, —
" I will send my dogs to lick your sores ! "

SHE TOLD HER BEADS.

SHE told her beads with downcast eyes,
  Within the ancient chapel dim;
 And ever as her fingers slim
Slipt o'er th' insensate ivories,
My rapt soul followed, spaniel-wise.
Ah, many were the beads she wore;
  But as she told them o'er and o'er,
They did not number all my sighs.
My heart was filled with unvoiced cries
  And prayers and pleadings unexpressed;
  But while I burned with Love's unrest,
She told her beads with downcast eyes.

LITTLE LUCY LANDMAN.

O H, the day has set me dreaming
   In a strange, half solemn way
Of the feelings I experienced
   On another long past day, —
Of the way my heart made music
   When the buds began to blow,
And o' little Lucy Landman
   Whom I loved long years ago.

It's in spring, the poet tells us,
   That we turn to thoughts of love,
And our hearts go out a-wooing
   With the lapwing and the dove.
But whene'er the soul goes seeking
   Its twin-soul, upon the wing,
I've a notion, backed by mem'ry,
   That it's love that makes the spring.

Lyrics of the Hearthside.

I have heard a robin singing
  When the boughs were brown and bare,
And the chilling hand of winter
  Scattered jewels through the air.
And in spite of dates and seasons,
  It was always spring, I know,
When I loved Lucy Landman
  In the days of long ago.

Ah, my little Lucy Landman,
  I remember you as well
As if 't were only yesterday
  I strove your thoughts to tell, —
When I tilted back your bonnet,
  Looked into your eyes so true,
Just to see if you were loving
  Me as I was loving you.

Ah, my little Lucy Landman
  It is true it was denied
You should see a fuller summer
  And an autumn by my side.

58

Little Lucy Landman.

But the glance of love's sweet sunlight
　　Which your eyes that morning gave
Has kept spring within my bosom,
　　Though you lie within the grave.

THE GOURD.

IN the heavy earth the miner
  Toiled and laboured day by day,
Wrenching from the miser mountain
  Brilliant treasure where it lay.
And the artist worn and weary
  Wrought with labour manifold
That the king might drink his nectar
  From a goblet made of gold.

On the prince's groaning table
  Mid the silver gleaming bright
Mirroring the happy faces
  Giving back the flaming light,
Shine the cups of priceless crystal
  Chased with many a lovely line,
Glowing now with warmer colour,
  Crimsoned by the ruby wine.

The Gourd.

In a valley sweet with sunlight,
  Fertile with the dew and rain,
Without miner's daily labour,
  Without artist's nightly pain,
There there grows the cup I drink from,
  Summer's sweetness in it stored,
And my lips pronounce a blessing
  As they touch an old brown gourd.

Why, the miracle at Cana
  In the land of Galilee,
Tho' it puzzles all the scholars,
  Is no longer strange to me.
For the poorest and the humblest
  Could a priceless wine afford,
If they 'd only dip up water
  With a sunlight-seasoned gourd.

So a health to my old comrade,
  And a song of praise to sing
When he rests inviting kisses
  In his place beside the spring.

Lyrics of the Hearth-side.

Give the king his golden goblets,
    Give the prince his crystal hoard;
But for me the sparkling water
    From a brown and brimming gourd!

The Knight.

THE KNIGHT.

OUR good knight, Ted, girds his broad-
    sword on
  (And he wields it well, I ween) ;
He 's on his steed, and away has gone
  To the fight for king and queen.
What tho' no edge the broadsword hath ?
What tho' the blade be made of lath ?
  'T is a valiant hand
  That wields the brand,
So, foeman, clear the path !

He prances off at a goodly pace ;
  'T is a noble steed he rides,
That bears as well in the speedy race
  As he bears in battle-tides.
What tho' 't is but a rocking-chair
That prances with this stately air ?
  'T is a warrior bold
  The reins doth hold,
Who bids all foes beware !

Lyrics of the Hearthside.

THOU ART MY LUTE.

THOU art my lute, by thee I sing, —
　My being is attuned to thee.
Thou settest all my words a-wing,
　And meltest me to melody.

Thou art my life, by thee I live,
　From thee proceed the joys I know;
Sweetheart, thy hand has power to give
　The meed of love — the cup of woe.

Thou art my love, by thee I lead
　My soul the paths of light along,
From vale to vale, from mead to mead,
　And home it in the hills of song.

My song, my soul, my life, my all,
　Why need I pray or make my plea,
Since my petition cannot fall;
　For I 'm already one with thee!

The Phantom Kiss.

THE PHANTOM KISS.

ONE night in my room, still and beamless,
  With will and with thought in eclipse,
I rested in sleep that was dreamless;
  When softly there fell on my lips

A touch, as of lips that were pressing
  Mine own with the message of bliss —
A sudden, soft, fleeting caressing,
  A breath like a maiden's first kiss.

I woke — and the scoffer may doubt me —
  I peered in surprise through the gloom;
But nothing and none were about me,
  And I was alone in my room.

Perhaps 't was the wind that caressed me
  And touched me with dew-laden breath;
Or, maybe, close-sweeping, there passed me
  The low-winging Angel of Death.

5   65

Lyrics of the Hearthside.

Some sceptic may choose to disdain it,
  Or one feign to read it aright;
Or wisdom may seek to explain it —
  This mystical kiss in the night.

But rather let fancy thus clear it:
  That, thinking of me here alone,
The miles were made naught, and, in spirit,
  Thy lips, love, were laid on mine own.

COMMUNION.

IN the silence of my heart,
   I will spend an hour with thee,
When my love shall rend apart
   All the veil of mystery :

All that dim and misty veil
   That shut in between our souls
When Death cried, " Ho, maiden, hail ! "
   And your barque sped on the shoals.

On the shoals?   Nay, wrongly said.
   On the breeze of Death that sweeps
Far from life, thy soul has sped
   Out into unsounded deeps.

I shall take an hour and come
   Sailing, darling, to thy side.
Wind nor sea may keep me from
   Soft communings with my bride.

Lyrics of the Hearthside.

I shall rest my head on thee
　　As I did long days of yore,
When a calm, untroubled sea
　　Rocked thy vessel at the shore.

I shall take thy hand in mine,
　　And live o'er the olden days
When thy smile to me was wine, —
　　Golden wine thy word of praise,

For the carols I had wrought
　　In my soul's simplicity ;
For the petty beads of thought
　　Which thine eyes alone could see.

Ah, those eyes, love-blind, but keen
　　For my welfare and my weal !
Tho' the grave-door shut between,
　　Still their love-lights o'er me steal.

I can see thee thro' my tears,
　　As thro' rain we see the sun.
What tho' cold and cooling years
　　Shall their bitter courses run, —

Communion.

I shall see thee still and be
   Thy true lover evermore,
And thy face shall be to me
   Dear and helpful as before.

Death may vaunt and Death may boast,
   But we laugh his pow'r to scorn;
He is but a slave at most, —
   Night that heralds coming morn.

I shall spend an hour with thee
   Day by day, my little bride.
True love laughs at mystery,
   Crying, " Doors of Death, fly wide."

MARE RUBRUM.

IN Life's Red Sea with faith I plant my feet,
    And wait the sound of that sustaining
        word
  Which long ago the men of Israel heard,
When Pharaoh's host behind them, fierce and
        fleet,
Raged on, consuming with revengeful heat.
    Why are the barrier waters still unstirred?—
    That struggling faith may die of hope de-
      ferred?
Is God not sitting in His ancient seat?

The billows swirl above my trembling limbs,
  And almost chill my anxious heart to doubt
    And disbelief, long conquered and defied.
But tho' the music of my hopeful hymns
  Is drowned by curses of the raging rout,
    No voice yet bids th' opposing waves
      divide!

In An English Garden.

IN AN ENGLISH GARDEN.

IN this old garden, fair, I walk to-day
 Heart-charmed with all the beauty of the
  scene :
 The rich, luxuriant grasses' cooling green,
The wall's environ, ivy-decked and gray,
The waving branches with the wind at play,
 The slight and tremulous blooms that show
  between,
 Sweet all : and yet my yearning heart doth
  lean
Toward Love's Egyptian flesh-pots far away.

Beside the wall, the slim Laburnum grows
 And flings its golden flow'rs to every breeze.
 But e'en among such soothing sights as
  these,
I pant and nurse my soul-devouring woes.
Of all the longings that our hearts wot of,
There is no hunger like the want of love !

THE CRISIS

A MAN of low degree was sore oppressed,
  Fate held him under iron-handed sway,
And ever, those who saw him thus distressed
  Would bid him bend his stubborn will and
    pray.
But he, strong in himself and obdurate,
Waged, prayerless, on his losing fight with
    Fate.

Friends gave his proffered hand their coldest
    clasp,
  Or took it not at all; and Poverty,
That bruised his body with relentless grasp,
  Grinned, taunting, when he struggled to be
    free.
But though with helpless hands he beat the air,
His need extreme yet found no voice in prayer.

The Crisis.

Then he prevailed; and forthwith snobbish
Fate,
    Like some whipped cur, came fawning at
    his feet;
Those who had scorned forgave and called
him great —
    His friends found out that friendship still
    was sweet.
But he, once obdurate, now bowed his head
In prayer, and trembling with its import, said:

" Mere human strength may stand ill-fortune's
frown;
    So I prevailed, for human strength was mine;
But from the killing pow'r of great renown,
    Naught may protect me save a strength divine.
Help me, O Lord, in this my trembling cause;
I scorn men's curses, but I dread applause ! "

THE CONQUERORS.

THE BLACK TROOPS IN CUBA.

ROUND the wide earth, from the red field
    your valour has won,
Blown with the breath of the far-speaking gun,
        Goes the word.
Bravely you spoke through the battle cloud heavy
    and dun.
Tossed though the speech toward the mist-
    hidden sun,
        The world heard.

Hell would have shrunk from you seeking it
    fresh from the fray,
Grim with the dust of the battle, and gray
        From the fight.

74

The Conquerors.

Heaven would have crowned you, with crowns
       not of gold but of bay,
Owning you fit for the light of her day,
       Men of night.

Far through the cycle of years and of lives that
       shall come,
There shall speak voices long muffled and dumb,
       Out of fear.
And through the noises of trade and the turbu-
       lent hum,
Truth shall rise over the militant drum,
       Loud and clear

Then on the cheek of the honester nation that
       grows,
All for their love of you, not for your woes,
       There shall lie
Tears that shall be to your souls as the dew to
       the rose ;
Afterward thanks, that the present yet knows
       Not to ply !

75

ALEXANDER CRUMMELL — DEAD.

BACK to the breast of thy mother,
    Child of the earth !
E'en her caress can not smother
What thou hast done.
Follow the trail of the westering sun
Over the earth.
Thy light and his were as one —
Sun, in thy worth.
Unto a nation whose sky was as night,
Camest thou, holily, bearing thy light :
And the dawn came,
In it thy fame
Flashed up in a flame.

Back to the breast of thy mother —
To rest.
Long hast thou striven ;

Alexander Crummell — Dead.

Dared where the hills by the lightning of heaven
    were riven ;
Go now, pure shriven.
Who shall come after thee, out of the clay —
Learned one and leader to show us the way?
Who shall rise up when the world gives the test?
Think thou no more of this —
Rest !

WHEN ALL IS DONE.

WHEN all is done, and my last word is
    said,
And ye who loved me murmur, " He is dead,"
Let no one weep, for fear that I should know,
And sorrow too that ye should sorrow so.

When all is done and in the oozing clay,
Ye lay this cast-off hull of mine away,
Pray not for me, for, after long despair,
The quiet of the grave will be a prayer.

For I have suffered loss and grievous pain,
The hurts of hatred and the world's disdain,
And wounds so deep that love, well-tried and
    pure,
Had not the pow'r to ease them or to cure.

When All is Done.

When all is done, say not my day is o'er,
And that thro' night I seek a dimmer shore:
Say rather that my morn has just begun, —
I greet the dawn and not a setting sun,
   When all is done.

THE POET AND THE BABY.

HOW'S a man to write a sonnet, can you
tell,—
How's he going to weave the dim, poetic
spell,—
  When a-toddling on the floor
  Is the muse he must adore,
And this muse he loves, not wisely, but too
  well?

Now, to write a sonnet, every one allows,
One must always be as quiet as a mouse;
  But to write one seems to me
  Quite superfluous to be,
When you've got a little sonnet in the house.

Just a dainty little poem, true and fine,
That is full of love and life in every line,
  Earnest, delicate, and sweet,
  Altogether so complete
That I wonder what's the use of writing mine.

DISTINCTION.

" I AM but clay," the sinner plead,
  Who fed each vain desire.
" Not only clay," another said,
  " But worse, for thou art mire."

THE SUM.

A LITTLE dreaming by the way,
 A little toiling day by day;
A little pain, a little strife,
A little joy, — and that is life.

A little short-lived summer's morn,
When joy seems all so newly born,
When one day's sky is blue above,
And one bird sings, — and that is love.

A little sickening of the years,
The tribute of a few hot tears
Two folded hands, the failing breath,
And peace at last, — and that is death.

Just dreaming, loving, dying so,
The actors in the drama go —
A flitting picture on a wall,
Love, Death, the themes; but is that all?

SONNET.

ON AN OLD BOOK WITH UNCUT LEAVES.

EMBLEM of blasted hope and lost desire,
    No finger ever traced thy yellow page
  Save Time's. Thou hast not wrought to
      noble rage
The hearts thou wouldst have stirred. Not any
    fire
Save sad flames set to light a funeral pyre
  Dost thou suggest. Nay, — impotent in age,
  Unsought, thou holdst a corner of the stage
And ceasest even dumbly to aspire.

How different was the thought of him that writ.
  What promised he to love of ease and wealth,
When men should read and kindle at his wit.
  But here decay eats up the book by stealth,
While it, like some old maiden, solemnly,
Hugs its incongruous virginity!

ON THE SEA WALL.

I SIT upon the old sea wall,
 And watch the shimmering sea,
Where soft and white the moonbeams fall,
 Till, in a fantasy,
Some pure white maiden's funeral pall
 The strange light seems to me.

The waters break upon the shore
 And shiver at my feet,
While I dream old dreams o'er and o'er,
 And dim old scenes repeat;
Tho' all have dreamed the same before,
 They still seem new and sweet.

The waves still sing the same old song
 That knew an elder time;
The breakers' beat is not more strong,
 Their music more sublime;
And poets thro' the ages long
 Have set these notes to rhyme.

On the Sea Wall.

But this shall not deter my lyre,
   Nor check my simple strain;
If I have not the old-time fire,
   I know the ancient pain:
The hurt of unfulfilled desire, —
   The ember quenched by rain.

I know the softly shining sea
   That rolls this gentle swell
Has snarled and licked its tongues at me
   And bared its fangs as well;
That 'neath its smile so heavenly,
   There lurks the scowl of hell!

But what of that?   I strike my string
   (For songs in youth are sweet);
I'll wait and hear the waters bring
   Their loud resounding beat;
Then, in her own bold numbers sing
   The Ocean's dear deceit!

Lyrics of the Hearthside.

TO A LADY PLAYING THE HARP.

THY tones are silver melted into sound,
　　And as I dream
I see no walls around,
　　But seem to hear
　　A gondolier
Sing sweetly down some slow Venetian stream.

Italian skies — that I have never seen —
　　I see above.
(Ah, play again, my queen;
　　Thy fingers white
　　Fly swift and light
And weave for me the golden mesh of love.)

Oh, thou dusk sorceress of the dusky eyes
　　And soft dark hair,
'T is thou that mak'st my skies

To a Lady Playing the Harp.

So swift to change
    To far and strange ;
But far and strange, thou still dost make them
        fair.

Now thou dost sing, and I am lost in thee
    As one who drowns
In floods of melody.
    Still in thy art
    Give me this part,
Till perfect love, the love of loving crowns.

CONFESSIONAL.

SEARCH thou my heart ;
 If there be guile,
It shall depart
 Before thy smile.

Search thou my soul ;
 Be there deceit,
'T will vanish whole
 Before thee, sweet.

Upon my mind
 Turn thy pure lens ;
Naught shalt thou find
 Thou canst not cleanse.

Confessional.

If I should pray,
   I scarcely know
In just what way
   My prayers would go.

So strong in me
   I feel love's leaven,
I 'd bow to thee
   As soon as Heaven !

MISAPPREHENSION.

OUT of my heart, one day, I wrote a song,
　　With my heart's blood imbued,
Instinct with passion, tremulously strong,
　　With grief subdued ;
　　Breathing a fortitude
　　Pain-bought.
And one who claimed much love for what I
　　wrought,
　　Read and considered it,
　　And spoke :
" Ay, brother, — tis well writ,
　　But where 's the joke ? "

Prometheus.

PROMETHEUS.

PROMETHEUS stole from Heaven the sacred
    fire
    And swept to earth with it o'er land and sea.
    He lit the vestal flames of poesy,
Content, for this, to brave celestial ire.

Wroth were the gods, and with eternal hate
    Pursued the fearless one who ravished Heaven
    That earth might hold in fee the perfect leaven
To lift men's souls above their low estate.

But judge you now, when poets wield the pen,
    Think you not well the wrong has been re-
        paired?
    'T was all in vain that ill Prometheus fared :
The fire has been returned to Heaven again !

Lyrics of the Hearthside.

We have no singers like the ones whose note
　　Gave challenge to the noblest warbler's song.
　　We have no voice so mellow, sweet, and strong
As that which broke from Shelley's golden throat.

The measure of our songs is our desires :
　　We tinkle where old poets used to storm.
　　We lack their substance tho' we keep their
　　　　form :
We strum our banjo-strings and call them lyres.

Love's Phases.

LOVE'S PHASES.

L OVE hath the wings of the butterfly,
    Oh, clasp him but gently,
Pausing and dipping and fluttering by
    Inconsequently.
Stir not his poise with the breath of a sigh;
Love hath the wings of the butterfly.

Love hath the wings of the eagle bold,
    Cling to him strongly —
What if the look of the world be cold,
    And life go wrongly?
Rest on his pinions, for broad is their fold;
Love hath the wings of the eagle bold.

Love hath the voice of the nightingale,
    Hearken his trilling —
List to his song when the moonlight is pale,—
    Passionate, thrilling.

Lyrics of the Hearthside.

Cherish the lay, ere the lilt of it fail;
Love hath the voice of the nightingale.

Love hath the voice of the storm at night,
    Wildly defiant.
Hear him and yield up your soul to his might,
    Tenderly pliant.
None shall regret him who heed him aright;
Love hath the voice of the storm at night.

For the Man who Fails.

FOR THE MAN WHO FAILS.

THE world is a snob, and the man who wins
    Is the chap for its money's worth:
And the lust for success causes half of the sins
    That are cursing this brave old earth.
For it 's fine to go up, and the world's applause
    Is sweet to the mortal ear;
But the man who fails in a noble cause
    Is a hero that 's no less dear.

'T is true enough that the laurel crown
    Twines but for the victor's brow;
For many a hero has lain him down
    With naught but the cypress bough.
There are gallant men in the losing fight,
    And as gallant deeds are done
As ever graced the captured height
    Or the battle grandly won.

Lyrics of the Hearthside.

We sit at life's board with our nerves highstrung,
   And we play for the stake of Fame,
And our odes are sung and our banners hung
   For the man who wins the game.
But I have a song of another kind
   Than breathes in these fame-wrought gales, —
An ode to the noble heart and mind
   Of the gallant man who fails!

The man who is strong to fight his fight,
   And whose will no front can daunt,
If the truth be truth and the right be right,
   Is the man that the ages want.
Tho' he fail and die in grim defeat,
   Yet he has not fled the strife,
And the house of Earth will seem more sweet
   For the perfume of his life.

Harriet Beecher Stowe.

HARRIET BEECHER STOWE.

SHE told the story, and the whole world wept
   At wrongs and cruelties it had not known
   But for this fearless woman's voice alone.
   She spoke to consciences that long had slept :
Her message, Freedom's clear reveille, swept
   From heedless hovel to complacent throne.
   Command and prophecy were in the tone
   And from its sheath the sword of justice leapt.
Around two peoples swelled a fiery wave,
   But both came forth transfigured from the
      flame.
Blest be the hand that dared be strong to save,
   And blest be she who in our weakness came —
   Prophet and priestess ! At one stroke she gave
   A race to freedom and herself to fame.

VAGRANTS.

LONG time ago, we two set out,
    My soul and I.
    I know not why,
For all our way was dim with doubt.
    I know not where
    We two may fare :
Though still with every changing weather,
We wander, groping on together.

We do not love, we are not friends,
    My soul and I.
    He lives a lie ;
Untruth lines every way he wends.
    A scoffer he
    Who jeers at me :
And so, my comrade and my brother,
We wander on and hate each other.

Vagrants.

Ay, there be taverns and to spare,
    Beside the road ;
    But some strange goad
Lets me not stop to taste their fare.
    Knew I the goal
    Toward which my soul
And I made way, hope made life fragrant :
But no.   We wander, aimless, vagrant !

A WINTER'S DAY.

ACROSS the hills and down the narrow ways,
    And up the valley where the free winds
        sweep,
  The earth is folded in an ermined sleep
That mocks the melting mirth of myriad Mays.
Departed her disheartening duns and grays,
    And all her crusty black is covered deep.
    Dark streams are locked in Winter's donjon-
        keep,
And made to shine with keen, unwonted rays.

O icy mantle, and deceitful snow!
    What world-old liars in your hearts ye are!
    Are there not still the darkened seam and scar
Beneath the brightness that you fain would show?
Come from the cover with thy blot and blur,
O reeking Earth, thou whited sepulchre!

My Little March Girl.

MY LITTLE MARCH GIRL.

COME to the pane, draw the curtain apart,
   There she is passing, the girl of my heart;
See where she walks like a queen in the street,
Weather-defying, calm, placid and sweet.
Tripping along with impetuous grace,
Joy of her life beaming out of her face,
Tresses all truant-like, curl upon curl,
Wind-blown and rosy, my little March girl.

Hint of the violet's delicate bloom,
Hint of the rose's pervading perfume!
How can the wind help from kissing her face,—
Wrapping her round in his stormy embrace?
But still serenely she laughs at his rout,
She is the victor who wins in the bout.
So may life's passions about her soul swirl,
Leaving it placid,— my little March girl.

Lyrics of the Hearthside.

What self-possession looks out of her eyes!
What are the wild winds, and what are the skies,
Frowning and glooming when, brimming with
     life,
Cometh the little maid ripe for the strife?
Ah! Wind, and bah! Wind, what might have
     you now?
What can you do with that innocent brow?
Blow, Wind, and grow, Wind, and eddy and
     swirl,
But bring her to me, Wind,— my little March
     girl.

Remembered.

REMEMBERED.

SHE sang, and I listened the whole song thro'.
    (It was sweet, so sweet, the singing.)
The stars were out and the moon it grew
From a wee soft glimmer way out in the blue
    To a bird thro' the heavens winging.

She sang, and the song trembled down to my
      breast, —
    (It was sweet, so sweet the singing.)
As a dove just out of its fledgling nest,
And, putting its wings to the first sweet test,
    Flutters homeward so wearily winging.

She sang and I said to my heart, "That song,
    That was sweet, so sweet i' the singing,
Shall live with us and inspire us long,
And thou, my heart, shalt be brave and strong
    For the sake of those words a-winging.

Lyrics of the Hearthside.

The woman died and the song was still.
    (It was sweet, so sweet, the singing.)
But ever I hear the same low trill,
Of the song that shakes my heart with a thrill,
    And goes forever winging.

Love Despoiled.

LOVE DESPOILED.

A S lone I sat one summer's day,
With mien dejected, Love came by ;
His face distraught, his locks astray,
So slow his gait, so sad his eye,
I hailed him with a pitying cry :

" Pray, Love, what has disturbed thee so ? "
Said I, amazed. " Thou seem 'st bereft ;
And see thy quiver hanging low,—
What, not a single arrow left ?
Pray, who is guilty of this theft ? "

Poor Love looked in my face and cried :
" No thief were ever yet so bold
To rob my quiver at my side.
But Time, who rules, gave ear to Gold,
And all my goodly shafts are sold."

THE LAPSE.

THIS poem must be done to-day;
    Then, I 'll e'en to it.
I must not dream my time away, —
    I 'm sure to rue it.
The day is rather bright, I know
    The Muse will pardon
My half-defection, if I go
    Into the garden.
It must be better working there, —
    I 'm sure it 's sweeter:
And something in the balmy air
    May clear my metre.

[*In the Garden.*]

Ah this is noble, what a sky!
    What breezes blowing!
The very clouds, I know not why,
    Call one to rowing.

The Lapse.

The stream will be a paradise
   To-day, I 'll warrant.
I know the tide that 's on the rise
   Will seem a torrent ;
I know just how the leafy boughs
   Are all a-quiver ;
I know how many skiffs and scows
   Are on the river.
I think I 'll just go out awhile
   Before I write it ;
When Nature shows us such a smile,
   We should n't slight it.
For Nature always makes desire
   By giving pleasure ;
And so 't will help me put more fire
   Into my measure.

[*On the River.*]

The river 's fine, I 'm glad I came,
   That poem 's teasing ;
But health is better far than fame,
   Though cheques are pleasing.

Lyrics of the Hearthside.

I don't know what I did it for, —
　　This air 's a poppy.
I 'm sorry for my editor, —
　　He 'll get no copy!

The Warrior's Prayer.

THE WARRIOR'S PRAYER.

L ONG since, in sore distress, I heard one
pray,
  " Lord, who prevailest with resistless might,
Ever from war and strife keep me away,
    My battles fight ! "

I know not if I play the Pharisee,
  And if my brother after all be right ;
But mine shall be the warrior's plea to thee —
    Strength for the fight.

I do not ask that thou shalt front the fray,
  And drive the warring foeman from my sight ;
I only ask, O Lord, by night, by day,
    Strength for the fight !

When foes upon me press, let me not quail
  Nor think to turn me into coward flight.
I only ask, to make mine arms prevail,
    Strength for the fight !

Lyrics of the Hearthside.

Still let mine eyes look ever on the foe,
   Still let mine armor case me strong and
      bright;
And grant me, as I deal each righteous blow,
      Strength for the fight!

And when, at eventide, the fray is done,
   My soul to Death's bedchamber do thou
      light,
And give me, be the field or lost or won,
      Rest from the fight!

FAREWELL TO ARCADY.

WITH sombre mien, the Evening gray
    Comes nagging at the heels of Day,
And driven faster and still faster
Before the dusky-mantled Master,
The light fades from her fearful eyes,
She hastens, stumbles, falls, and dies.

Beside me Amaryllis weeps ;
The swelling tears obscure the deeps
Of her dark eyes, as, mistily,
The rushing rain conceals the sea.
Here, lay my tuneless reed away, —
I have no heart to tempt a lay.

I scent the perfume of the rose
Which by my crystal fountain grows.
In this sad time, are roses blowing?
And thou, my fountain, art thou flowing,

Lyrics of the Hearthside.

While I who watched thy waters spring
Am all too sad to smile or sing?
Nay, give me back my pipe again,
It yet shall breathe this single strain:
    Farewell to Arcady!

THE VOICE OF THE BANJO.

IN a small and lonely cabin out of noisy
     traffic's way,
Sat an old man, bent and feeble, dusk of face,
     and hair of gray,
And beside him on the table, battered, old, and
     worn as he,
Lay a banjo, droning forth this reminiscent
     melody:

"Night is closing in upon us, friend of mine,
     but don't be sad;
Let us think of all the pleasures and the joys
     that we have had.
Let us keep a merry visage, and be happy till
     the last,
Let the future still be sweetened with the honey
     of the past.

" For I speak to you of summer nights upon the
    yellow sand,
When the Southern moon was sailing high and
    silvering all the land ;
And if love tales were not sacred, there 's a tale
    that I could tell
Of your many nightly wanderings with a dusk
    and lovely belle.

" And I speak to you of care-free songs when
    labour's hour was o'er,
And a woman waiting for your step outside the
    cabin door,
And of something roly-poly that you took upon
    your lap,
While you listened for the stumbling, hesitating
    words, ' Pap, pap.'

" I could tell you of a 'possum hunt across the
    wooded grounds,
I could call to mind the sweetness of the baying
    of the hounds,

The Voice of the Banjo.

You could lift me up and smelling of the tim-
      ber that 's in me,
Build again a whole green forest with the mem-
      'ry of a tree.

" So the future cannot hurt us while we keep
      the past in mind,
What care I for trembling fingers, — what care
      you that you are blind?
Time may leave us poor and stranded, circum-
      stance may make us bend;
But they 'll only find us mellower, won't they,
      comrade? — in the end."

THE STIRRUP CUP.

COME, drink a stirrup cup with me,
    Before we close our rouse.
You 're all aglow with wine, I know :
    The master of the house,
    Unmindful of our revelry,
    Has drowned the carking devil care,
    And slumbers in his chair.

Come, drink a cup before we start ;
    We 've far to ride to-night.
And Death may take the race we make,
    And check our gallant flight :
    But even he must play his part,
    And tho' the look he wears be grim,
    We 'll drink a toast to him !

For Death,— a swift old chap is he,
    And swift the steed He rides.
He needs no chart o'er main or mart,

116

The Stirrup Cup.

For no direction bides.
So, come, a final cup with me,
And let the soldiers' chorus swell, —
To hell with care, to hell !

A CHOICE.

THEY please me not — these solemn songs
    That hint of sermons covered up.
'T is true the world should heed its wrongs,
    But in a poem let me sup,
Not simples brewed to cure or ease
Humanity's confessed disease,
But the spirit-wine of a singing line,
    Or a dew-drop in a honey cup !

HUMOUR AND DIALECT.

THEN AND NOW.

THEN.

HE loved her, and through many years,
    Had paid his fair devoted court,
Until she wearied, and with sneers
Turned all his ardent love to sport.

That night within his chamber lone,
He long sat writing by his bed
A note in which his heart made moan
For love ; the morning found him dead.

NOW.

Like him, a man of later day
Was jilted by the maid he sought,
And from her presence turned away,
Consumed by burning, bitter thought.

Lyrics of the Hearthside.

He sought his room to write — a curse
Like him before and die, I ween.
Ah no, he put his woes in verse,
And sold them to a magazine.

AT CHESHIRE CHEESE.

WHEN first of wise old Johnson taught,
    My youthful mind its homage brought,
And made the pond'rous, crusty sage
The object of a noble rage.

Nor did I think (How dense we are !)
That any day, however far,
Would find me holding, unrepelled,
The place that Doctor Johnson held !

But change has come and time has moved,
And now, applauded, unreproved,
I hold, with pardonable pride,
The place that Johnson occupied.

Conceit !   Presumption !   What is this?
You surely read my words amiss ;
Like Johnson I, — a man of mind !
How could you ever be so blind?

Lyrics of the Hearthside.

No.   At the ancient " Cheshire Cheese,"
Blown hither by some vagrant breeze,
To dignify my shallow wit,
In Doctor Johnson's seat I sit !

My Corn-Cob Pipe.

MY CORN-COB PIPE.

MEN may sing of their Havanas, elevating
to the stars
The real or fancied virtues of their foreign-made
cigars ;
But I worship Nicotina at a different sort of
shrine,
And she sits enthroned in glory in this corn-cob
pipe of mine.

It's as fragrant as the meadows when the clover
is in bloom ;
It's as dainty as the essence of the daintiest
perfume ;
It's as sweet as are the orchards when the fruit
is hanging ripe,
With the sun's warm kiss upon them — is this
corn-cob pipe.

Lyrics of the Hearthside.

Thro' the smoke about it clinging, I delight its
    form to trace,
Like an oriental beauty with a veil upon her
    face ;
And my room is dim with vapour as a church
    when censers sway,
As I clasp it to my bosom — in a figurative way.

It consoles me in misfortune and it cheers me
    in distress,
And it proves a warm partaker of my pleasures
    in success ;
So I hail it as a symbol, friendship's true and
    worthy type,
And I press my lips devoutly to my corn-cob
    pipe.

In August.

IN AUGUST.

WHEN August days are hot an' dry,
    When burning copper is the sky,
I'd rather fish than feast or fly
In airy realms serene and high.

I'd take a suit not made for looks,
Some easily digested books,
Some flies, some lines, some bait, some hooks,
Then would I seek the bays and brooks.

I would eschew mine every task,
In Nature's smiles my soul should bask,
And I methinks no more could ask,
Except — perhaps — one little flask.

In case of accident, you know,
Or should the wind come on to blow,
Or I be chilled or capsized, so,
A flask would be the only go.

Lyrics of the Hearthside.

Then could I spend a happy time, —
A bit of sport, a bit of rhyme
(A bit of lemon, or of lime,
To make my bottle's contents prime).

When August days are hot an' dry,
I won't sit by an' sigh or die,
I 'll get my bottle (on the sly)
And go ahead, and fish, and lie !

THE DISTURBER.

OH, what shall I do? I am wholly upset;
    I am sure I 'll be jailed for a lunatic yet.
I 'll be out of a job — it 's the thing to expect
When I 'm letting my duty go by with neglect.
You may judge the extent and degree of my
      plight
When I 'm thinking all day and a-dreaming all
      night,
And a-trying my hand at a rhyme on the sly,
All on account of a sparkling eye.

There are those who say men should be strong,
      well-a-day!
But what constitutes strength in a man? Who
      shall say?
I am strong as the most when it comes to the
      arm.
I have aye held my own on the playground or
      farm.

Lyrics of the Hearthside.

And when I've been tempted, I haven't been
  weak;
But now — why, I tremble to hear a maid speak.
I used to be bold, but now I've grown shy,
And all on account of a sparkling eye.

There once was a time when my heart was
  devout,
But now my religion is open to doubt.
When parson is earnestly preaching of grace,
My fancy is busy with drawing a face,
Thro' the back of a bonnet most piously plain;
' I draw it, redraw it, and draw it again.'
While the songs and the sermon unheeded go
  by, —
All on account of a sparkling eye.

Oh, dear little conjurer, give o'er your wiles,
It is easy for you, you're all blushes and
  smiles:
But, love of my heart, I am sorely perplexed;
I am smiling one minute and sighing the next;

The Disturber.

And if it goes on, I 'll drop hackle and flail,
And go to the parson and tell him my tale.
I warrant he 'll find me a cure for the sigh
That you 're aye bringing forth with the glance
    of your eye.

EXPECTATION.

YOU 'LL be wonderin' whut's de reason
    I 's a grinnin' all de time,
An' I guess you t'ink my sperits
    Mus' be feelin' mighty prime.
Well, I 'fess up, I is tickled
    As a puppy at his paws.
But you need n't think I 's crazy,
    I ain' laffin' 'dout a cause.

You 's a wonderin' too, I reckon,
    Why I does n't seem to eat,
An' I notice you a lookin'
    Lak you felt completely beat
When I 'fuse to tek de bacon,
    An' don' settle on de ham.
Don' you feel no feah erbout me,
    Jes' keep eatin', an' be ca'm.

Fu' I 's waitin' an' I 's watchin'
    'Bout a little t'ing I see —

Expectation.

D' othah night I 's out a walkin'
　　An' I passed a 'simmon tree.
Now I 's whettin' up my hongry,
　　An' I 's laffin' fit to kill,
Fu' de fros' done turned de 'simmons,
　　An' de possum 's eat his fill.

He done go'ged hisse'f owdacious,
　　An' he stayin' by de tree !
Don' you know, ol' Mistah Possum
　　Dat you gittin' fat fu' me?
'Tain't no use to try to 'spute it,
　　'Case I knows you 's gittin' sweet
Wif dat 'simmon flavoh thoo you,
　　So I 's waitin' fu' yo' meat.

An' some ebenin' me an' Towsah
　　Gwine to come an' mek a call,
We jes' drap in onexpected
　　Fu' to shek yo' han', dat's all.
Oh, I knows dat you 'll be tickled,
　　Seems lak I kin see you smile,
So pu'haps I mought pu'suade you
　　Fu' to visit us a while.

131

LOVER'S LANE.

SUMMAH night an' sighin' breeze,
  'Long de lovah's lane ;
Frien'ly, shadder-mekin' trees,
  'Long de lovah's lane.
White folks' wo'k all done up gran' —
Me an' 'Mandy han'-in-han'
Struttin' lak we owned de lan',
  'Long de lovah's lane.

Owl a-settin' 'side de road,
  'Long de lovah's lane,
Lookin' at us lak he knowed
  Dis uz lovah's lane.
Go on, hoot yo' mou'nful tune,
You ain' nevah loved in June,
An' come hidin' f'om de moon
  Down in lovah's lane.

Lover's Lane.

Bush it ben' an' nod an' sway,
   Down in lovah's lane,
Try'n' to hyeah me whut I say
   'Long de lovah's lane.
But I whispahs low lak dis,
An' my 'Mandy smile huh bliss —
Mistah Bush he shek his fis',
   Down in lovah's lane.

Whut I keer ef day is long,
   Down in lovah's lane.
I kin allus sing a song
   'Long de lovah's lane.
An' de wo'ds I hyeah an' say
Meks up fu' de weary day
W'en I 's strollin' by de way,
   Down in lovah's lane.

An' dis t'ought will allus rise
   Down in lovah's lane :
Wondah whethah in de skies
   Dey 's a lovah's lane.

133

Lyrics of the Hearthside.

Ef dey ain't, I tell you true,
'Ligion do look mighty blue,
'Cause I do' know whut I 'd do
   'Dout a lovah's lane.

PROTEST.

WHO say my hea't ain't true to you?
    Dey bettah heish dey mouf.
I knows I loves you thoo an' thoo
    In watah time er drouf.
I wush dese people 'd stop dey talkin',
Don't mean no mo' dan chicken's squawkin':
I guess I knows which way I 's walkin',
    I knows de norf f'om souf.

I does not love Elizy Brown,
    I guess I knows my min'.
You allus try to tek me down
    Wid evaht'ing you fin'.
Ef dese hyeah folks will keep on fillin'
Yo' haid wid nonsene, an' you 's willin'
I bet some day dey 'll be a killin'
    Somewhaih along de line.

Lyrics of the Hearthside.

O' cose I buys de gal ice-cream,
    Whut else I gwine to do?
I knows jes' how de t'ing 'u'd seem
    Ef I 'd be sho't wid you.
On Sunday, you 's at chu'ch a-shoutin',
Den all de week you go 'roun' poutin' —
I 's mighty tiahed o' all dis doubtin',
    I tell you cause I 's true.

Hymn

HYMN.

O LI'L' lamb out in de col',
  De Mastah call you to de fol',
    O li'l' lamb!
He hyeah you bleatin' on de hill;
Come hyeah an' keep yo' mou'nin' still,
    O li'l' lamb!

De Mastah sen' de Shepud fo'f;
He wandah souf, he wandah no'f,
    O li'l' lamb!
He wandah eas', he wandah wes';
De win' a-wrenchin' at his breas',
    O li'l' lamb!

Oh, tell de Shepud whaih you hide;
He want you walkin' by his side,
    O li'l' lamb!
He know you weak, he know you so';
But come, don' stay away no mo',
    O li'l' lamb!

Lyrics of the Hearthside.

An' af'ah while de lamb he hyeah
De Shepud's voice a-callin' cleah —
    Sweet li'l' lamb !
He answah f'om de brambles thick,
" O Shepud, I 's a-comin' quick " —
    O li'l' lamb !

LITTLE BROWN BABY.

L ITTLE brown baby wif spa'klin' eyes,
 Come to yo' pappy an' set on his knee.
What you been doin', suh — makin' san' pies?
 Look at dat bib — you 's ez du'ty ez me.
Look at dat mouf — dat 's merlasses, I bet;
 Come hyeah, Maria, an' wipe off his han's.
Bees gwine to ketch you an' eat you up yit,
 Bein' so sticky an sweet — goodness lan's!

Little brown baby wif spa'klin' eyes,
 Who 's pappy's darlin' an' who 's pappy's
  chile?
Who is it all de day nevah once tries
 Fu' to be cross, er once loses dat smile?
Whah did you git dem teef? My, you 's a
  scamp!
 Whah did dat dimple come f'om in yo' chin?
Pappy do' know yo — I b'lieves you 's a tramp;
 Mammy, dis hyeah 's some ol' straggler
  got in!

Lyrics of the Hearthside.

Let 's th'ow him outen de do' in de san',
   We do' want stragglers a-layin' 'roun' hyeah;
Let 's gin him 'way to de big buggah-man;
   I know he 's hidin' erroun' hyeah right neah.
Buggah-man, buggah-man, come in de do',
   Hyeah's a bad boy you kin have fu' to eat.
Mammy an' pappy do' want him no mo',
   Swaller him down f'om his haid to his feet!

Dah, now, I t'ought dat you 'd hug me up close.
   Go back, ol' buggah, you sha'n't have dis
     boy.
He ain't no tramp, ner no straggler, of co'se;
   He 's pappy's pa'dner an' playmate an' joy.
Come to you' pallet now — go to yo' res';
   Wisht you could allus know ease an' cleah
     skies;
Wisht you could stay jes' a chile on my breas' —
   Little brown baby wif spa'klin' eyes!

Time to Tinker 'Roun' !

TIME TO TINKER 'ROUN'!

SUMMAH 'S nice, wif sun a-shinin',
  Spring is good wif greens and grass,
An' dey 's some t'ings nice 'bout wintah,
  Dough hit brings de freezin' blas';
But de time dat is de fines,
  Whethah fiel's is green er brown,
Is w'en de rain 's a-po'in'
  An' dey 's time to tinker 'roun.'

Den you men's de mule's ol' ha'ness,
  An' you men's de broken chair.
Hummin' all de time you 's wo'kin'
  Some ol' common kind o' air.
Evah now an' then you looks out,
  Tryin' mighty ha'd to frown,
But you cain't, you 's glad hit 's rainin',
  An' dey 's time to tinker 'roun'.

Lyrics of the Hearthside.

Oh, you 'ten's lak you so anxious
    Evah time it so't o' stops.
W'en hit goes on, den you reckon
    Dat de wet 'll he'p de crops.
But hit ain't de crops you's aftah ;
    You knows w'en de rain comes down
Dat 's hit 's too wet out fu' wo'kin',
    An' dey 's time to tinker 'roun'.

Oh, dey 's fun inside de co'n-crib,
    An' dey 's laffin' at de ba'n ;
An' dey 's allus some one jokin',
    Er some one to tell a ya'n.
Dah 's a quiet in yo' cabin,
    Only fu' de rain's sof' soun' ;
So you 's mighty blessed happy
    W'en dey 's time to tinker 'roun' !

The Real Question.

THE REAL QUESTION.

FOLKS is talkin' 'bout de money, 'bout de
    silvah an' de gold ;
All de time de season 's changin' an' de days is
    gittin' cold.
An' dey 's wond'rin' 'bout de metals, whethah
    we 'll have one er two.
While de price o' coal is risin' an' dey 's two
    months' rent dat 's due.

Some folks says dat gold 's de only money dat is
    wuff de name,
Den de othahs rise an' tell 'em dat dey ought
    to be ashame,
An' dat silvah is de only thing to save us f'om
    de powah
Of de gold-bug ragin' 'roun' an' seekin' who he
    may devowah.

Lyrics of the Hearthside.

Well, you folks kin keep on shoutin' wif yo'
    gold er silvah cry,
But I tell you people hams is sceerce an' fowls
    is roostin' high.
An' hit ain't de so't o' money dat is pesterin'
    my min',
But de question I want answehed 's how to get
    at any kin'!

Jilted.

JILTED.

LUCY done gone back on me,
　　Dat 's de way wif life.
Evaht'ing was movin' free,
　　T'ought I had my wife.
Den some dahky comes along,
Sings my gal a little song,
Since den, evaht'ing 's gone wrong,
　　Evah day dey 's strife.

Did n't answeh me to-day,
　　W'en I called huh name,
Would you t'ink she 'd ac' dat way
　　W'en I ain't to blame?
Dat 's de way dese women do,
W'en dey fin's a fellow true,
Den dey 'buse him thoo an' thoo;
　　Well, hit 's all de same.

Lyrics of the Hearthside.

Somep'n 's wrong erbout my lung,
   An' I 's glad hit 's so.
Doctah says 'at I 'll die young,
   Well, I wants to go !
Whut 's de use o' livin' hyeah,
W'en de gal you loves so deah,
Goes back on you clean an' cleah —
   I sh'd like to know?

The News.

THE NEWS.

WHUT dat you whisperin' keepin' f'om me?
    Don't shut me out 'cause I's ol' an'
    can't see.
Somep'n' 's gone wrong dat's a-causin' you
    dread, —
Don't be afeared to tell — Whut! mastah dead?

Somebody brung de news early to-day, —
One of de sojers he led, do you say?
Did n't he foller whah ol' mastah led?
How kin he live w'en his leadah is dead?

Let me lay down awhile, dah by his bed;
I wants to t'ink, — hit ain't cleah in my head: —
Killed while a-leadin' his men into fight, —
Dat's whut you said, ain't it, did I hyeah right?

Lyrics of the Hearthside.

Mastah, my mastah, dead dah in de fiel'?
Lif' me up some, — dah, jes' so I kin kneel.
I was too weak to go wid him, dey said,
Well, now I'll — fin' him — so — mastah is
     dead.

Yes, suh, I's comin' ez fas' ez I kin, —
'T was kin' o' da'k, but hit's lightah agin:
P'omised yo' pappy I'd allus tek keer
Of you, — yes, mastah, — I's follerin', — hyeah!

Chrismus on the Plantation.

CHRISMUS ON THE PLANTATION.

IT was Chrismus Eve, I mind hit fu' a
    mighty gloomy day —
Bofe de weathah an' de people — not a one
    of us was gay;
Cose you 'll t'ink dat 's mighty funny 'twell I
    try to mek hit cleah,
Fu' a da'ky 's allus happy when de holidays is
    neah.

But we was n't, fu' dat mo'nin' Mastah 'd tol' us
    we mus' go,
He 'd been payin' us sence freedom, but he
    could n't pay no mo';
He wa'n't nevah used to plannin' 'fo' he got so
    po' an' ol',
So he gwine to give up tryin', an' de homestead
    mus' be sol'.

Lyrics of the Hearthside.

I kin see him stan'in' now erpon de step ez
     cleah ez day,
Wid de win' a·kind o' fondlin' thoo his haih all
     thin an' gray;
An' I 'membah how he trimbled when he said,
     "It 's ha'd fu' me,
Not to mek yo' Chrismus brightah, but I 'low
     it wa'n't to be."

All de women was a-cryin', an' de men, too, on
     de sly,
An' I noticed somep'n shinin' even in ol' Mas-
     tah's eye.
But we all stood still to listen ez ol' Ben come
     f'om de crowd
An' spoke up, a-try'n' to steady down his voice
     and mek it loud : —

"Look hyeah, Mastah, I 's been servin' you' fu'
     lo ! dese many yeahs,
An' now, sence we 's got freedom an' you 's kind
     o' po', hit 'pears

Chrismus on the Plantation.

Dat you want us all to leave you 'cause you
    don't t'ink you can pay.
Ef my membry has n't fooled me, seem dat
    whut I hyead you say.

" Er in othah wo'ds, you wants us to fu'git dat
    you 's been kin',
An' ez soon ez you is he'pless, we 's to leave
    you hyeah behin'.
Well, ef dat 's de way dis freedom ac's on peo-
    ple, white er black,
You kin jes' tell Mistah Lincum fu' to tek his
    freedom back.

" We gwine wo'k dis ol' plantation fu' whatevah
    we kin git,
Fu' I know hit did suppo't us, an' de place kin
    do it yit.
Now de land is yo's, de hands is ouahs, an' I
    reckon we 'll be brave,
An' we 'll bah ez much ez you do w'en we has
    to scrape an' save."

Lyrics of the Hearthside.

Ol' Mastah stood dah trimblin', but a-smilin'
    thoo his teahs,
An' den hit seemed jes' nachul-like, de place
    fah rung wid cheahs,
An' soon ez dey was quiet, some one sta'ted
    sof' an' low :
"Praise God," an' den we all jined in, "from
    whom all blessin's flow!"

Well, dey was n't no use tryin', ouah min's was
    sot to stay,
An' po' ol' Mastah could n't plead ner baig, ner
    drive us 'way,
An' all at once, hit seemed to us, de day was
    bright agin,
So evahone was gay dat night, an' watched de
    Chrismus in.

ANGELINA.

WHEN de fiddle gits to singin' out a ol'
    Vahginny reel,
An' you 'mence to feel a ticklin' in yo' toe an'
    in yo' heel;
Ef you t'ink you got 'uligion an' you wants to
    keep it, too,
You jes' bettah tek a hint an' git yo'self clean
    out o' view.
Case de time is mighty temptin' when de chune
    is in de swing,
Fu' a darky, saint or sinner man, to cut de
    pigeon-wing.
An' you couldn't he'p f'om dancin' ef yo' feet
    was boun' wif twine,
When Angelina Johnson comes a-swingin' down
    de line.

Don't you know Miss Angelina? She's de
    da'lin' of de place.
W'y, dey ain't no high-toned lady wif sich man-
    nahs an' sich grace.

Lyrics of the Hearthside.

She kin move across de cabin, wif its planks all
    rough an' wo';
Jes' de same 's ef she was dancin' on ol' mistus'
    ball-room flo'.
Fact is, you do' see no cabin — evaht'ing you
    see look grand,
An' dat one ol' squeaky fiddle soun' to you jes'
    lak a ban';
Cotton britches look lak broadclof an' a linsey
    dress look fine,
When Angelina Johnson comes a-swingin' down
    de line.

Some folks say dat dancin 's sinful, an' de blessed
    Lawd, dey say,
Gwine to purnish us fu' steppin' w'en we hyeah
    de music play.
But I tell you I don' b'lieve it, fu' de Lawd is
    wise and good,
An' he made de banjo's metal an' he made de
    fiddle's wood,
An' he made de music in dem, so I don' quite
    t'ink he 'll keer

Angelina.

Ef our feet keeps time a little to de melodies
    we hyeah.
W'y, dey's somep'n' downright holy in de way
    our faces shine,
When Angelina Johnson comes a-swingin' down
    de line.

Angelina steps so gentle, Angelina bows so low,
An' she lif' huh sku't so dainty dat huh shoetop
    skacely show :
An' dem teef o' huh'n a-shinin', ez she tek you
    by de han' —
Go 'way, people, d' ain't anothah sich a lady in
    de lan' !
When she's movin' thoo de figgers er a-dancin'
    by huhse'f,
Folks jes' stan' stock-still a-sta'in', an' dey mos'
    nigh hol's dey bref ;
An' de young mens, dey's a-sayin', "I's gwine
    mek dat damsel mine,"
When Angelina Johnson comes a-swingin' down
    de line.

FOOLIN' WID DE SEASONS.

SEEMS lak folks is mighty curus
    In de way dey t'inks an' ac's.
Dey jes' spen's dey days a-mixin'
    Up de t'ings in almanacs.
Now, I min' my nex' do' neighbour, —
    He 's a mighty likely man,
But he nevah t'inks o' nuffin
    'Ceptin' jes' to plot an' plan.

All de wintah he was plannin'
    How he 'd gethah sassafras
Jes' ez soon ez evah Springtime
    Put some greenness in de grass.
An' he 'lowed a little soonah
    He could stan' a coolah breeze
So 's to mek a little money
    F'om de sugah-watah trees.

156

Foolin' wid de Seasons.

In de summah, he'd be waihin'
    Out de linin' of his soul,
Try'n' to ca'ci'late an' fashion
    How he'd git his wintah coal:
An' I b'lieve he got his jedgement
    Jes' so tuckahed out an' thinned
Dat he t'ought a robin's whistle
    Was de whistle of de wind.

Why won't folks gin up dey plannin',
    An' jes' be content to know
Dat dey's gittin' all dat's fu' dem
    In de days dat come an' go?
Why won't folks quit movin' forrard?
    Ain't hit bettah jes' to stan'
An' be satisfied wid livin'
    In de season dat's at han'?

Hit's enough fu' me to listen
    W'en de birds is singin' 'roun',
'Dout a-guessin' whut'll happen
    W'en de snow is on de groun'.

157

Lyrics of the Hearthside.

In de Springtime an' de summah,
    I lays sorrer on de she'f;
An' I knows ol' Mistah Wintah
    Gwine to hustle fu' hisse'f.

We been put hyeah fu' a pu'pose,
    But de questun dat has riz
An' made lots o' people diffah
    Is jes' whut dat pu'pose is.
Now, accordin' to my reas'nin',
    Hyeah 's de p'int whaih I 's arriv,
Sence de Lawd put life into us,
    We was put hyeah fu' to live !

MY SORT O' MAN.

I DON'T believe in 'ristercrats
    An' never did, you see;
The plain ol' homelike sorter folks
    Is good enough fur me.
O' course, I don't desire a man
    To be too tarnal rough,
But then, I think all folks should know
    When they air nice enough.

Now there is folks in this here world,
    From peasant up to king,
Who want to be so awful nice
    They overdo the thing.
That's jest the thing that makes me sick,
    An' quicker 'n a wink
I set it down that them same folks
    Ain't half so good 's you think.

Lyrics of the Hearthside.

I like to see a man dress nice,
  In clothes becomin' too;
I like to see a woman fix
  As women orter to do;
An' boys an' gals I like to see
  Look fresh an' young an' spry,—
We all must have our vanity
  An' pride before we die.

But I jedge no man by his clothes,—
  Nor gentleman nor tramp;
The man that wears the finest suit
  May be the biggest scamp,
An' he whose limbs air clad in rags
  That make a mournful sight,
In life's great battle may have proved
  A hero in the fight.

I don't believe in 'ristercrats;
  I like the honest tan
That lies upon the heathful cheek
  An' speaks the honest man;

My Sort o' Man.

I like to grasp the brawny hand
    That labor's lips have kissed,
For he who has not labored here
    Life's greatest pride has missed:

The pride to feel that yore own strength
    Has cleaved fur you the way
To heights to which you were not born,
    But struggled day by day.
What though the thousands sneer an' scoff,
    An' scorn yore humble birth?
Kings are but puppets; you are king
    By right o' royal worth.

The man who simply sits an' waits
    Fur good to come along,
Ain't worth the breath that one would take
    To tell him he is wrong.
Fur good ain't flowin' round this world
    Fur every fool to sup;
You 've got to put yore see-ers on,
    An' go an' hunt it up.

Lyrics of the Hearthside.

Good goes with honesty, I say,
    To honour an' to bless;
To rich an' poor alike it brings
    A wealth o' happiness.
The 'ristercrats ain't got it all.
    Fur much to their su'prise,
That's one of earth's most blessed things
    They can't monopolize.

Possum.

POSSUM.

EF dey's anyt'ing dat riles me
  An' jes' gits me out o' hitch,
Twell I want to tek my coat off,
  So 's to r'ar an' t'ar an' pitch,
Hit 's to see some ign'ant white man
  'Mittin' dat owdacious sin —
W'en he want to cook a possum
  Tekin' off de possum's skin.

W'y, dey ain't no use in talkin',
  Hit jes' hu'ts me to de hea't
Fu' to see dem foolish people
  Th'owin' 'way de fines' pa't.
W'y, dat skin is jes' ez tendah
  An' ez juicy ez kin be ;
I knows all erbout de critter—
  Hide an' haih — don't talk to me !

163

Lyrics of the Hearthside.

Possum skin is jes lak shoat skin;
   Jes' you swinge an' scrope it down,
Tek a good sha'p knife an' sco' it,
   Den you bake it good an' brown.
Huh-uh! honey, you 's so happy
   Dat yo' thoughts is 'mos' a sin
When you 's settin' dah a-chawin'
   On dat possum's cracklin' skin.

White folks t'ink dey know 'bout eatin',
   An' I reckon dat dey do
Sometimes git a little idee
   Of a middlin' dish er two;
But dey ain't a t'ing dey knows of
   Dat I reckon cain't be beat
W'en we set down at de table
   To a unskun possum's meat!

On the Road.

ON THE ROAD.

I 'S boun' to see my gal to-night —
  Oh, lone de way, my dearie !
De moon ain't out, de stars ain't bright —
  Oh, lone de way, my dearie !
Dis hoss o' mine is pow'ful slow,
But when I does git to yo' do'
Yo' kiss 'll pay me back, an' mo',
  Dough lone de way, my dearie.

De night is skeery-lak an' still —
  Oh, lone de way, my dearie !
'Cept fu' dat mou'nful whippo'will —
  Oh, lone de way, my dearie !
De way so long wif dis slow pace,
' T 'u'd seem to me lak savin' grace
Ef you was on a nearer place,
  Fu' lone de way, my dearie.

165

Lyrics of the Hearthside.

I hyeah de hootin' of de owl —
   Oh, lone de way, my dearie !
I wish dat watch-dog would n't howl —
   Oh, lone de way, my dearie !
An' evaht'ing, bofe right an' lef',
Seem p'int'ly lak hit put itse'f
In shape to skeer me half to def —
   Oh, lone de way, my dearie !

I whistles so 's I won't be feared —
   Oh lone de way, my dearie !
But anyhow I 's kin' o' skeered,
   Fu' lone de way, my dearie.
De sky been lookin' mighty glum,
But you kin mek hit lighten some,
Ef you 'll jes' say you 's glad I come,
   Dough lone de way, my dearie.

A Death Song.

A DEATH SONG.

LAY me down beneaf de willers in de grass,
    Whah de branch 'll go a-singin' as it pass.
  An' w'en I 's a-layin' low,
  I kin hyeah it as it go
Singin', "Sleep, my honey, tek yo' res' at las'."

Lay me nigh to whah hit meks a little pool,
An' de watah stan's so quiet lak an' cool,
    Whah de little birds in spring,
    Ust to come an' drink an' sing,
An' de chillen waded on dey way to school.

Let me settle w'en my shouldahs draps dey load
Nigh enough to hyeah de noises in de road ;
    Fu' I t'ink de las' long res'
    Gwine to soothe my sperrit bes'
Ef I 's layin' 'mong de t'ings I 's allus knowed.

A BACK–LOG SONG.

DE axes has been ringin' in de woods de
blessid day,
An' de chips has been a-fallin' fa' an' thick ;
Dey has cut de bigges' hick'ry dat de mules kin
tote away,
An' dey's laid hit down and soaked it in de
crik.
Den dey tuk hit to de big house an' dey piled
de wood erroun'
In de fiah-place f'om ash-flo' to de flue,
While ol' Ezry sta'ts de hymn dat evah yeah
has got to soun'
When de back-log fus' commence a-bu'nin'
thoo.

Ol' Mastah is a-smilin' on de da'kies f'om de
hall,
Ol' Mistus is a-stannin' in de do',

A Back-Log Song.

An' de young folks, males an' misses, is a-tryin',
 one an' all,
  Fu' to mek us feel hit 's Chrismus time fu' sho'.
An' ouah hea'ts are full of pleasure, fu' we
 know de time is ouahs
  Fu' to dance er do jes' whut we wants to do.
An' dey ain't no ovahseer an' no othah kind o'
 powahs
  Dat kin stop us while dat log is bu'nin thoo.

Dey 's a-wokin' in de qua'tahs a-preparin' fu' de
 feas',
  So de little pigs is feelin' kind o' shy.
De chickens ain't so trus'ful ez dey was, to say
 de leas',
  An' de wise ol' hens is roostin' mighty high.
You could n't git a gobblah fu' to look you in de
 face —
  I ain't sayin' whut de tu'ky 'spects is true ;
But hit 's mighty dange'ous trav'lin' fu' de
 critters on de place
  F'om de time dat log commence a bu'nin'
  thoo.

Lyrics of the Hearthside.

Some one's tunin' up his fiddle dah, I hyeah a
    banjo's ring,
      An', bless me, dat's de tootin' of a ho'n!
Now dey'll evah one be runnin' dat has got a
    foot to fling,
      An' dey'll dance an' frolic on f'om now 'twell
      mo'n.
Plunk de banjo, scrap de fiddle, blow dat ho'n
    yo' level bes',
      Keep yo' min' erpon de chune an' step it
      true.
Oh, dey ain't no time fu' stoppin' an' dey ain't
    no time fu' res',
      Fu' hit's Chrismus an' de back-log's bu'nin'
      thoo!

LULLABY.

BEDTIME 'S come fu' little boys.
Po' little lamb.
Too tiahed out to make a noise,
Po' little lamb.
You gwine t' have to-morrer sho' ?
Yes, you tole me dat befo',
Don't you fool me, chile, no mo',
Po' little lamb.

You been bad de livelong day,
Po' little lamb.
Th'owin' stones an' runnin' 'way,
Po' little lamb.
My, but you 's a-runnin' wil',
Look jes' lak some po' folks chile ;
Mam' gwine whup you atter while,
Po' little lamb.

Come hyeah ! you mos' tiahed to def,
Po' little lamb.

Played yo'se'f clean out o' bref,
    Po' little lamb.
See dem han's now — sich a sight !
Would you evah b'lieve dey 's white ?
Stan' still twell I wash 'em right,
    Po' little lamb.

Jes' cain't hol' yo' haid up straight,
    Po' little lamb.
Had n't oughter played so late,
    Po' little lamb.
Mammy do' know whut she 'd do,
Ef de chillun's all lak you ;
You 's a caution now fu' true,
    Po' little lamb.

Lay yo' haid down in my lap,
    Po' little lamb.
Y' ought to have a right good slap,
    Po' little lamb.
You been runnin' roun' a heap.
Shet dem eyes an' don't you peep,
Dah now, dah now, go to sleep,
    Po' little lamb.

The Photograph.

THE PHOTOGRAPH.

SEE dis pictyah in my han'?
   Dat's my gal;
Ain't she purty? goodness lan'!
   Huh name Sal.
Dat's de very way she be —
Kin' o' tickles me to see
Huh a-smilin' back at me.

She sont me dis photygraph
   Jes' las' week;
An' aldough hit made me laugh —
   My black cheek
Felt somethin' a-runnin' queer;
Bless yo' soul, it was a tear
Jes' f'om wishin' she was here.

Often when I's all alone
   Layin' here,
I git t'inkin' 'bout my own
   Sallie dear;

173

Lyrics of the Hearthside.

How she say dat I 's huh beau,
An' hit tickles me to know
Dat de gal do love me so.

Some bright day I 's goin' back,
   Fo' de la !
An' ez sho' 's my face is black,
   Ax huh pa
Fu' de blessed little miss
Who 's a-smilin' out o' dis
Pictyah, lak she wan'ed a kiss !

JEALOUS.

HYEAH come Cæsar Higgins,
    Don't he think he's fine?
Look at dem new riggin's
Ain't he tryin' to shine?
Got a standin' collar
An' a stove-pipe hat,
I 'll jes' bet a dollar
Some one gin him dat.

Don't one o' you mention,
Nothin' 'bout his cloes,
Don't pay no attention,
Er let on you knows
Dat he 's got 'em on him,
Why, 't 'll mek him sick,
Jes go on an' sco'n him,
My, ain't dis a trick!

175

Lyrics of the Hearthside.

Look hyeah, whut's he doin'
Lookin' t' othah way?
Dat ere move 's a new one,
Some one call him, " Say ! "
Can't you see no pusson —
Puttin' on you' airs,
Sakes alive, you 's wuss'n
Dese hyeah millionaires.

Need n't git so flighty,
Case you got dat suit.
Dem cloes ain't so mighty, —
Second hand to boot,
I 's a-tryin' to spite you !
Full of jealousy !
Look hyeah, man, I 'll fight you,
Don't you fool wid me !

Parted.

PARTED.

DE breeze is blowin' 'cross de bay.
    My lady, my lady;
De ship hit teks me far away,
    My lady, my lady.
Ole Mas' done sol' me down de stream;
Dey tell me 't ain't so bad 's hit seem,
    My lady, my lady.

O' co'se I knows dat you 'll be true,
    My lady, my lady;
But den I do' know whut to do,
    My lady, my lady.
I knowed some day we 'd have to pa't,
But den hit put' nigh breaks my hea't,
    My lady, my lady.

Lyrics of the Hearthside.

De day is long, de night is black,
    My lady, my lady;
I know you 'll wait twell I come back,
    My lady, my lady.
I 'll stan' de ship, I 'll stan' de chain,
But I 'll come back, my darlin' Jane,
    My lady, my lady.

Jes' wait, jes' b'lieve in whut I say,
    My lady, my lady;
D' ain't nothin' dat kin keep me 'way,
    My lady, my lady.
A man 's a man, an' love is love;
God knows ouah hea'ts, my little dove;
He 'll he'p us f'om his th'one above,
    My lady, my lady.

TEMPTATION.

I DONE got 'uligion, honey, an' I 's happy ez
    a king;
Evahthing I see erbout me 's jes' lak sunshine
    in de spring;
An' it seems lak I do' want to do anothah blessid
    thing
But jes' run an' tell de neighbours, an' to shout
    an' pray an' sing.

I done shuk my fis' at Satan, an' I 's gin de worl'
    my back;
I do' want no hendrin' causes now a-both'rin'
    in my track;
Fu' I 's on my way to glory, an' I feels too sho'
    to miss.
W'y, dey ain't no use in sinnin' when 'uligion 's
    sweet ez dis.

179

Lyrics of the Hearthside.

Talk erbout a man backslidin' w'en he 's on de
    gospel way ;
No, suh, I done beat de debbil, an' Temptation 's
    los' de day.
Gwine to keep my eyes right straight up, gwine
    to shet my eahs, an' see
Whut ole projick Mistah Satan 's gwine to try to
    wuk on me.

Listen, whut dat soun' I hyeah dah ? 'tain't no
    one commence to sing ;
It 's a fiddle ; git erway dah ! don' you hyeah
    dat blessid thing ?
W'y, dat 's sweet ez drippin' honey, 'cause, you
    knows, I draws de bow,
An' when music 's sho' 'nough music, I 's de one
    dat 's sho' to know.

W'y, I 's done de double shuffle, twell a body
    could n't res',
Jes' a-hyeahin' Sam de fiddlah play dat chune
    his level bes' ;

Temptation.

I could cut a mighty caper, I could gin a mighty
      fling
Jes' right now, I 's mo' dan suttain I could cut
      de pigeon wing.

Look hyeah, whut's dis I 's been sayin'? whut
      on urf 's tuk holt o' me?
Dat ole music come nigh runnin' my 'uligion up
      a tree !
Cleah out wif dat dah ole fiddle, don' you try
      dat trick agin ;
Did n't think I could be tempted, but you lak to
      made me sin !

POSSUM TROT.

I'VE journeyed 'roun' consid'able, a-seein'
    men an' things,
An' I 've learned a little of the sense that meetin'
    people brings ;
But in spite of all my travellin', an' of all I think
    I know,
I 've got one notion in my head, that I can't git
    to go ;
An' it is that the folks I meet in any other spot
Ain't half so good as them I knowed back home
    in Possum Trot.

I know you 've never heerd the name, it ain't a
    famous place,
An' I reckon ef you'd search the map you could
    n't find a trace
Of any sich locality as this I 've named to you ;
But never mind, I know the place, an' I love it
    dearly too.

Possum Trot.

It don't make no pretensions to bein' great or
    fine,
The circuses don't come that way, they ain't no
    railroad line.
It ain't no great big city, where the schemers
    plan an' plot,
But jest a little settlement, this place called
    Possum Trot.

But don't you think the folks that lived in that
    outlandish place
Were ignorant of all the things that go for sense
    or grace.
Why, there was Hannah Dyer, you may search
    this teemin' earth
An' never find a sweeter girl, er one o' greater
    worth ;
An' Uncle Abner Williams, a-leanin' on his staff,
It seems like I kin hear him talk, an' hear his
    hearty laugh.
His heart was big an' cheery as a sunny acre lot,
Why, that 's the kind o' folks we had down there
    at Possum Trot.

Lyrics of the Hearthside.

Good times? Well, now, to suit my taste, —
    an' I 'm some hard to suit, —
There ain't been no sich pleasure sence, an'
    won't be none to boot,
With huskin' bees in Harvest time, an' dances
    later on,
An' singin' school, an taffy pulls, an' fun from
    night till dawn.
Revivals come in winter time, baptizin's in the
    spring,
You 'd ought to seen those people shout, an'
    heerd 'em pray an' sing;
You 'd ought to 've heard ole Parson Brown
    a-throwin' gospel shot
Among the saints an' sinners in the days of
    Possum Trot.

We live up in the city now, my wife was bound
    to come ;
I hear aroun' me day by day the endless stir
    an' hum.
I reckon that it done me good, an' yet it done
    me harm, .

Possum Trot.

That oil was found so plentiful down there on
    my ole farm.
We 've got a new-styled preacher, our church is
    new-styled too,
An' I 've come down from what I knowed to
    rent a cushioned pew.
But often when I 'm settin' there, it 's foolish,
    like as not,
To think of them ol' benches in the church at
    Possum Trot.

I know that I 'm ungrateful, an' sich thoughts
    must be a sin,
But I find myself a wishin' that the times was
    back agin.
With the huskin's an' the frolics, an' the joys I
    used to know,
When I lived at the settlement, a dozen years
    ago.
I don't feel this way often, I 'm scarcely ever
    glum,
For life has taught me how to take her chances
    as they come.

Lyrics of the Hearthside.

But now an' then my mind goes back to that
    ol' buryin' plot,
That holds the dust of some I loved, down there
    at Possum Trot.

Dely.

DELY.

JES' lak toddy wahms you thoo'
    Sets yo' haid a reelin',
Meks you ovah good and new,
    Dat 's de way I 's feelin'.
Seems to me hit 's summah time,
    Dough hit 's wintah reely,
I 's a feelin' jes' dat prime —
    An' huh name is Dely.

Dis hyeah love 's a cu'rus thing,
    Changes 'roun' de season,
Meks you sad or meks you sing,
    'Dout no urfly reason.
Sometimes I go mopin' 'roun',
    Den agin I 's leapin';
Sperits allus up an' down
    Even when I 's sleepin'.

Lyrics of the Hearthside.

Fu' de dreams comes to me den,
    An' dey keeps me pitchin',
Lak de apple dumplin's w'en
    Bilin' in de kitchen.
Some one sot to do me hahm,
    Tryin' to ovahcome me,
Ketchin' Dely by de ahm
    So 's to tek huh f'om me.

Mon, you bettah b'lieve I fights
    (Dough hit 's on'y seemin') ;
I 's a hittin' fu' my rights
    Even w'en I 's dreamin'.
But I 'd let you have 'em all,
    Give 'em to you freely,
Good an' bad ones, great an' small,
    So 's you leave me Dely.

Dely got dem meltin' eyes,
    Big an' black an' tendah.
Dely jes' a lady-size,
    Delikit an' slendah.

Dely.

Dely brown ez brown kin be
    An' huh haih is curly;
Oh, she look so sweet to me, —
    Bless de precious girlie!

Dely brown ez brown kin be,
    She ain' no mullatter;
She pure cullud, — don' you see
    Dat's jes' whut's de mattah?
Dat's de why I love huh so,
    D' ain't no mix about huh,
Soon's you see huh face you know
    D' ain't no chanst to doubt huh.

Folks dey go to chu'ch an' pray
    So's to git a blessin'.
Oomph, dey bettah come my way,
    Dey could lu'n a lesson.
Sabbaf day I don' go fu',
    Jes' to see my pigeon;
I jes' sets an' looks at huh,
    Dat's enuff 'uligion.

BREAKING THE CHARM.

CAUGHT Susanner whistlin'; well,
   It's most nigh too good to tell.
'Twould 'a' b'en too good to see
Ef it had n't b'en fur me,
Comin' up so soft an' sly
That she didn' hear me nigh.
I was pokin' 'round that day,
An' ez I come down the way,
First her whistle strikes my ears, —
Then her gingham dress appears;
So with soft step up I slips.
Oh, them dewy, rosy lips!
Ripe ez cherries, red an' round,
Puckered up to make the sound.
She was lookin' in the spring,
Whistlin' to beat anything, —
"Kitty Dale" er "In the Sweet."
I was jest so mortal beat

Breaking the Charm.

That I can't quite ricoleck
What the toon was, but I 'speck
'T was some hymn er other, fur
Hymny things is jest like her.
Well she went on fur awhile
With her face all in a smile,
An' I never moved, but stood
Stiller 'n a pieçe o' wood —
Would n't wink ner would n't stir,
But a-gazin' right at her,
Tell she turns an' sees me — my !
Thought at first she 'd try to fly.
But she blushed an' stood her ground.
Then, a-slyly lookin' round,
She says : "Did you hear me, Ben ? "
" Whistlin' woman, crowin' hen,"
Says I, lookin' awful stern.
Then the red commenced to burn
In them cheeks o' hern.   Why, la !
Reddest red you ever saw —
Pineys wa'n't a circumstance.
You 'd 'a' noticed in a glance
She was pow'rful shamed an' skeart ;

Lyrics of the Hearthside.

But she looked so sweet an' peart,
That a idee struck my head;
So I up an' slowly said:
"Woman whistlin' brings shore harm,
Jest one thing 'll break the charm."
"And what's that?" "Oh my!" says I,
"I don't like to tell you." "Why?"
Says Susanner. "Well, you see
It would kinder fall on me."
Course I knowed that she'd insist, —
So I says: "You must be kissed
By the man that heard you whistle;
Everybody says that this 'll
Break the charm and set you free
From the threat'nin' penalty."
She was blushin' fit to kill,
But she answered, kinder still:
"I don't want to have no harm,
Please come, Ben, an' break the charm."
Did I break that charm? — oh, well,
There's some things I must n't tell.
I remember, afterwhile,
Her a-sayin' with a smile:

Breaking the Charm.

" Oh, you quit, — you sassy dunce,
You jest caught me whistlin' *once*."
Ev'ry sence that when I hear
Some one whistlin' kinder clear,
I most break my neck to see
Ef it 's Susy ; but, dear me,
I jest find I 've b'en to chase
Some blamed boy about the place.
Dad 's b'en noticin' my way,
An' last night I heerd him say :
" We must send fur Dr. Glenn,
Mother ; somethin 's wrong with Ben ! "

HUNTING SONG.

TEK a cool night, good an' cleah,
    Skiff o' snow upon de groun';
Jes' 'bout fall-time o' de yeah
    W'en de leaves is dry an' brown;
Tek a dog an' tek a axe,
    Tek a lantu'n in yo' han',
Step light whah de switches cracks,
    Fu' dey 's huntin' in de lan'.
Down thoo de valleys an' ovah de hills,
    Into de woods whah de 'simmon-tree grows,
Wakin' an' skeerin' de po' whippo'wills,
    Huntin' fu' coon an' fu' 'possum we goes.

Blow dat ho'n dah loud an' strong,
    Call de dogs an' da'kies neah;
Mek its music cleah an' long,
    So de folks at home kin hyeah.

194

Hunting Song.

Blow it twell de hills an' trees
      Sen's de echoes tumblin' back;
Blow it twell de back'ard breeze
      Tells de folks we 's on de track.
Coons is a-ramblin' an' 'possums is out;
  Look at dat dog; you could set on his tail!
Watch him now — steady, — min' — what you 's
    about,
    Bless me, dat animal 's got on de trail!

Listen to him ba'kin' now!
      Dat means bus'ness, sho 's you bo'n;
Ef he 's struck de scent I 'low
      Dat ere 'possum 's sholy gone.
Knowed dat dog fu' fo'teen yeahs,
      An' I nevah seed him fail
W'en he sot dem flappin' eahs
      An' went off upon a trail.
Run, Mistah 'Possum, an' run, Mistah Coon,
  No place is safe fu' yo' ramblin' to-night;
Mas' gin' de lantu'n an' God gin de moon,
    An' a long hunt gins a good appetite.

Lyrics of the Hearthside.

Look hyeah, folks, you hyeah dat change?
　　Dat ba'k is sha'per dan de res'.
Dat ere soun' ain't nothin' strange, —
　　Dat dog 's talked his level bes'.
Somep'n' 's treed, I know de soun'.
　　Dah now, — wha 'd I tell you? see!
Dat ere dog done run him down;
　　Come hyeah, he'p cut down dis tree.
Ah, Mistah 'Possum, we got you at las' —
　Need n't play daid, laying dah on de groun';
Fros' an' de 'simmons has made you grow fas', —
　Won't he be fine when he 's roasted up brown!

A Letter.

A LETTER.

DEAR Miss Lucy: I been t'inkin' dat
    I 'd write you long fo' dis,
But dis writin' 's mighty tejous, an' you know
    jes' how it is.
But I 's got a little lesure, so I teks my pen in
    han'
Fu' to let you know my feelin's since I retched
    dis furrin' lan'.
I 's right well, I 's glad to tell you (dough dis
    climate ain't to blame),
An' I hopes w'en dese lines reach you, dat dey 'll
    fin' yo' se'f de same.
Cose I 'se feelin' kin' o' homesick — dat 's ez
    nachul ez kin be,
W'en a feller 's mo'n th'ee thousand miles across
    dat awful sea.
(Don't you let nobidy fool you 'bout de ocean
    bein' gran';

Lyrics of the Hearthside.

If you want to see de billers, you jes' view dem
    f'om de lan'.)
'Bout de people? We been t'inkin' dat all
    white folks was alak;
But dese Englishmen is diffunt, an' dey's curus
    fu' a fac'.
Fust, dey's heavier an' redder in dey make-up
    an' dey looks,
An' dey don't put salt nor pepper in a blessed
    t'ing dey cooks!
W'en dey gin you good ol' tu'nips, ca'ots, pa's-
    nips, beets, an' sich,
Ef dey ain't some one to tell you, you cain't
    'stinguish which is which.
W'en I t'ought I'se eatin' chicken — you may
    b'lieve dis hyeah's a lie —
But de waiter beat me down dat I was eatin'
    rabbit pie.
An' dey'd t'ink dat you was crazy — jes' a reg'-
    lar ravin' loon,
Ef you'd speak erbout a 'possum or a piece o'
    good ol' coon.
O, hit's mighty nice, dis trav'lin', an' I's kin' o'
    glad I come.

A Letter.

But, I reckon, now I 's willin' fu' to tek my way
    back home.
I done see de Crystal Palace, an' I 's hyeahd
    dey string-band play,
But I has n't seen no banjos layin' nowhahs
    roun' dis way.
Jes' gin ol' Jim Bowles a banjo, an' he 'd not go
    very fu',
'Fo' he 'd outplayed all dese fiddlers, wif dey
    flourish and dey stir.
Evahbiddy dat I 's met wif has been monst'ous
    kin' an' good ;
But I t'ink I 'd lak it better to be down in Jones's
    wood,
Where we ust to have sich frolics, Lucy, you an'
    me an' Nelse,
Dough my appetite 'ud call me, ef dey was n't
    nuffin else.
I 'd jes' lak to have some sweet-pertaters roasted
    in de skin ;
I 's a-longin' fu' my chittlin's an' my mustard
    greens ergin ;
I 's a-wishin' fu' some buttermilk, an' co'n braid,
    good an' brown,

An' a drap o' good ol' bourbon fu' to wash my
    feelin's down !

An' I 's comin' back to see you jes' as ehly as I
    kin,

So you better not go spa'kin' wif dat wuffless
    scoun'el Quin !

Well, I reckon, I mus' close now ; write ez soon
    's dis reaches you ;

Gi' my love to Sister Mandy an' to Uncle
    Isham, too.

Tell de folks I sen' 'em howdy ; gin a kiss to
    pap an' mam ;

Closin' I is, deah Miss Lucy,

            Still Yo' Own True-Lovin' SAM.

P. S.   Ef you cain't mek out dis letter, lay it by
    erpon de she'f,

      An' when I git home, I 'll read, it, darlin',
        to you my own se'f.

CHRISMUS IS A–COMIN'.

BONES a-gittin' achy,
   Back a-feelin' col',
Han's a-growin' shaky,
Jes' lak I was ol'.
Fros' erpon de meddah
Lookin' mighty white ;
Snowdraps lak a feddah
Slippin' down at night.
Jes' keep t'ings a-hummin'
Spite o' fros' an' showahs,
Chrismus is a-comin'
An' all de week is ouahs.

Little mas' a-axin',
"Who is Santy Claus? "
Meks it kin' o' taxin'
Not to brek de laws.
Chillun 's pow'ful tryin'

Lyrics of the Hearthside.

To a pusson's grace
W'en dey go a pryin'
Right on th'oo you' face
Down ermong yo' feelin's;
Jes' 'pears lak dat you
Got to change you' dealin's
So 's to tell 'em true.

An' my pickaninny—
Dreamin' in his sleep!
Come hyeah, Mammy Jinny,
Come an' tek a peep.
Ol' Mas' Bob an' Missis
In dey house up daih
Got no chile lak dis is,
D' ain't none anywhaih.
Sleep, my little lammy,
Sleep, you little limb,
He do' know whut mammy
Done saved up fu' him.

Dey 'll be banjo pickin',
Dancin' all night thoo.

Chrismuś is A-comin'.

Dey'll be lots o' chicken,
Plenty tukky, too.
Drams to wet yo' whistles
So's to drive out chills.
Whut I keer fu' drizzles
Fallin' on de hills?
Jes' keep t'ings a-hummin'
Spite o' col' an' showahs,
Chrismus day's a-comin',
An' all de week is ouahs.

A CABIN TALE.

THE YOUNG MASTER ASKS FOR A STORY.

WHUT you say, dah? huh, uh! chile,
  You's enough to dribe me wile.
Want a sto'y; jes' hyeah dat!
Whah' 'll I git a sto'y at?
Di'n' I tell you th'ee las' night?
Go 'way, honey, you ain't right.
I got somep'n' else to do,
'Cides jes' tellin' tales to you.
Tell you jes' one? Lem me see
Whut dat one's a-gwine to be.
When you 's ole, yo membry fails;
Seems lak I do' know no tales.
Well, set down dah in dat cheer,
Keep still ef you wants to hyeah.
Tek dat chin up off yo' han's,
Set up nice now. Goodness lan's!

A Cabin Tale.

Hol' yo'se'f up lak yo' pa.
Bet nobidy evah saw
Him scrunched down lak you was den —
High-tone boys meks high-tone men.

Once dey was a ole black bah,
Used to live 'roun' hyeah somewhah
In a cave.   He was so big
He could ca'y off a pig
Lak you picks a chicken up,
Er yo' leetles' bit o' pup.
An' he had two gread big eyes,
Jes' erbout a saucer's size.
Why, dey looked lak balls o' fiah
Jumpin' 'roun' erpon a wiah
W'en dat bah was mad; an' laws!
But you ought to seen his paws!
Did I see 'em?   How you 'spec
I 's a-gwine to ricollec'
Dis hyeah ya'n I 's try'n' to spin
Ef you keeps on puttin' in?
You keep still an' don't you cheep
Less I 'll sen' you off to sleep.

Lyrics of the Hearthside.

Dis hyeah bah 'd go trompin' 'roun'
Eatin' evahthing he foun';
No one could n't have a fa'm
But dat bah 'u'd do 'em ha'm;
And dey could n't ketch de scamp.
Anywhah he wan'ed to tramp,
Dah de scoun'el 'd mek his track,
Do his du't an' come on back.
He was sich a sly ole limb,
Traps was jes' lak fun to him.

Now, down neah whah Mistah Bah
Lived, dey was a weasel dah;
But dey was n't fren's a-tall
Case de weasel was so small.
An' de bah 'u'd, jeṣ' fu' sass,
Tu'n his nose up w'en he 'd pass.
Weasels 's small o' cose, but my!
Dem air animiles is sly.
So dis hyeah one says, says he,
"I 'll jes' fix dat bah, you see."
So he fixes up his plan
An' hunts up de fa'merman.

A Cabin Tale.

When de fa'mer see him come,
He 'mence lookin' mighty glum,
An' he ketches up a stick;
But de weasel speak up quick:
"Hol' on, Mistah Fa'mer man,
I wan' 'splain a little plan.
Ef you waits, I 'll tell you whah
An' jes' how to ketch ol' Bah.
But I tell yow now you mus'
Gin me one fat chicken fus'."
Den de man he scratch his haid,
Las' he say, "I 'll mek de trade."
So de weasel et his hen,
Smacked his mouf and says, "Well, den,
Set yo' trap an' bait ternight,
An' I 'll ketch de bah all right."
Den he ups an' goes to see
Mistah Bah, an' says, says he:
"Well, fren' Bah, we *ain't* been fren's,
But ternight ha'd feelin' 'en's.
Ef you ain't too proud to steal,
We kin git a splendid meal.
Cose I would n't come to you,

But it mus' be done by two ;
Hit's a trap, but we kin beat
All dey tricks an' git de meat."
" Cose I 's wif you," says de bah,
" Come on, weasel, show me whah."
Well, dey trots erlong ontwell
Dat air meat beginned to smell
In de trap.   Den weasel say :
" Now you put yo' paw dis way
While I hol' de spring back so,
Den you grab de meat an' go."
Well, de bah he had to grin
Ez he put his big paw in,
Den he juked up, but — kerbing !
Weasel done let go de spring.
" Dah now," says de weasel, " dah,
I done cotched you, Mistah Bah ! "
O, dat bah did sno't and spout,
Try'n' his bestes' to git out,
But de weasel say, " Goo'-bye !
Weasel small, but weasel sly."
Den he tu'ned his back an' run
Tol' de fa'mer whut he done.

A Cabin Tale.

So de fa'mer come down dah,
Wif a axe and killed de bah.

    Dah now, ain't dat sto'y fine?
Run erlong now, nevah min'.
Want some mo', you rascal, you?
No, suh! no, suh! dat 'll do.

AT CANDLE-LIGHTIN' TIME.

WHEN I come in f'om de co'n-fiel' aftah
wo'kin' ha'd all day,
It's amazin' nice to fin' my suppah all erpon de
way;
An' it's nice to smell de coffee bubblin' ovah in
de pot,
An' it's fine to see de meat a-sizzlin' teasin'-
lak an' hot.

But when suppah-time is ovah, an' de t'ings is
cleahed away;
Den de happy hours dat foller are de sweetes'
of de day.
When my co'ncob pipe is sta'ted, an' de smoke
is drawin' prime,
My ole 'ooman says, " I reckon, Ike, it's can-
dle-lightin' time."

At Candle-Lightin' Time.

Den de chillun snuggle up to me, an' all com-
    mence to call,
"Oh, say, daddy, now it's time to mek de
    shadders on de wall."
So I puts my han's togethah — evah daddy
    knows de way, —
An' de chillun snuggle closer roun' ez I begin
    to say : —

"Fus' thing, hyeah come Mistah Rabbit; don'
    you see him wo'k his eahs?
Huh, uh! dis mus' be a donkey, — look,
    how innercent he 'pears !
Dah's de ole black swan a-swimmin' — ain't she
    got a' awful neck?
Who's dis feller dat's a-comin'? Why, dat's
    ole dog Tray, I 'spec' ! "

Dat's de way I run on, tryin' fu' to please 'em
    all I can ;
Den I hollahs, "Now be keerful — dis hyeah
    las' 's de buga-man ! "

An' dey runs an' hides dey faces; dey ain't
    skeered — dey's lettin' on:
But de play ain't raaly ovah twell dat buga-
    man is gone.

So I jes' teks up my banjo, an' I plays a little
    chune,
An' you see dem haids come peepin' out to
    listen mighty soon.
Den my wife says, " Sich a pappy fu' to give
    you sich a fright !
Jes' you go to baid, an' leave him: say yo'
    prayers an' say good-night."

Whistling Sam.

WHISTLING SAM.

I HAS hyeahd o' people dancin' an' I's
hyeahd o' people singin'.
An' I's been 'roun' lots of othahs dat could keep
de banjo ringin';
But of all de whistlin' da'kies dat have lived an'
died since Ham,
De whistlin'est I evah seed was ol' Ike Bates's
Sam.
In de kitchen er de stable, in de fiel' er mowin'
hay,
You could hyeah dat boy a-whistlin' pu'ty nigh
a mile erway, —
Puck'rin' up his ugly features 'twell you could n't
see his eyes,
Den you 'd hyeah a soun' lak dis un f'om dat
awful puckah rise:

Lyrics of the Hearthside.

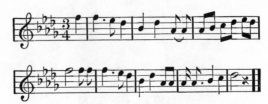

When dey had revival meetin' an' de Lawd's
    good grace was flowin'
On de groun' dat needed wat'rin' whaih de
    seeds of good was growin',
While de othahs was a-singin' an' a-shoutin'
    right an' lef',
You could hyeah dat boy a-whistlin' kin' o' sof'
    beneaf his bref:

Whistling Sam.

At de call fu' colo'ed soldiers, Sam enlisted
'mong de res'

Wid de blue o' Gawd's great ahmy wropped
about his swellin' breas',

An' he laffed an' whistled loudah in his youfful
joy an' glee

Dat de govament would let him he'p to mek
his people free.

Daih was lots o' ties to bin' him, pappy, mammy,
an' his Dinah,—

Dinah, min' you, was his sweethea't, an' dey
was n't nary finah;

But he lef' 'em all, I tell you, lak a king he
ma'ched away,

Try'n' his level bes' to whistle, happy, solemn,
choky, gay:

Lyrics of the Hearthside.

To de front he went an' bravely fought de foe
an' kep' his sperrit,

An' his comerds said his whistle made 'em
strong when dey could hyeah it.

When a saber er a bullet cut some frien' o' his'n
down,

An' de time 'u'd come to trench him an' de
boys 'u'd gethah 'roun',

An' dey could n't sta't a hymn-tune, mebbe
none o' dem 'u'd keer,

Sam 'u'd whistle "Sleep in Jesus," an' he
knowed de Mastah 'd hyeah.

In de camp, all sad discouraged, he would cheer
de hea'ts of all,

When above de soun' of labour dey could hyeah
his whistle call:

Whistling Sam.

When de cruel wah was ovah an' de boys come
    ma'chin' back,

Dey was shouts an' cries an' blessin's all erlong
    dey happy track,

An' de da'kies all was happy; souls an' bodies
    bofe was freed.

Why, hit seemed lak de Redeemah mus' 'a' been
    on earf indeed.

Dey was gethahed all one evenin' jes' befo' de
    cabin do',

When dey hyeahd somebody whistlin' kin' o' sof'
    an' sweet an' low.

Dey could n't see de whistlah, but de hymn was
    cleah and ca'm,

An' dey all stood daih a-listenin' ontwell Dinah
    shouted, "Sam!"

An' dey seed a little da'ky way off yandah thoo
    de trees

Wid his face all in a puckah mekin' jes' sich
    soun's ez dese :

HOW LUCY BACKSLID.

DE times is mighty stirrin' 'mong de people up ouah way,
Dey 'sputin' an' dey argyin' an' fussin' night an'
day;
An' all dis monst'ous trouble dat hit meks me
tiahed to tell
Is 'bout dat Lucy Jackson dat was sich a mighty
belle.

She was de preachah's favoured, an' he tol' de
chu'ch one night
Dat she travelled thoo de cloud o' sin a-bearin'
of a light;
But, now, I 'low he t'inkin' dat she mus' 'a' los'
huh lamp,
Case Lucy done backslided an' dey trouble in
de camp.

218

How Lucy Backslid.

Huh daddy wants to beat huh, but huh mammy
    daihs him to,
Fu' she lookin' at de question f'om a ooman's
    pint o' view;
An' she say dat now she would n't have it dif-
    f'ent ef she could;
Dat huh darter only acted jes' lak any othah
    would.

Cose you know w'en women argy, dey is mighty
    easy led
By dey hea'ts an' don't go foolin' 'bout de
    reasons of de haid.
So huh mammy laid de law down (she ain'
    reckernizin' wrong),
But you got to mek erlowance fu' de cause dat
    go along.

Now de cause dat made Miss Lucy fu' to th'ow
    huh grace away
I 's afeard won't baih no 'spection w'en hit come
    to jedgement day;

Lyrics of the Hearthside.

Do' de same t'ing been a-wo'kin' evah sence de
    worl' began, —
De ooman disobeyin' fu' to 'tice along a man.

Ef you 'tended de revivals which we held de
    wintah pas',
You kin rickolec' dat convuts was a-comin' thick
    an' fas' ;
But dey ain't no use in talkin', dey was all lef'
    in de lu'ch
W'en ol' Mis' Jackson's dartah foun' huh peace
    an' tuk de chu'ch.

W'y, she shouted ovah evah inch of Ebenezah's
    flo' ;
Up into de preachah's pulpit an' f'om dah down
    to de do' ;
Den she hugged an' squeezed huh mammy, an'
    she hugged an' kissed huh dad,
An' she struck out at huh sistah, people said,
    lak she was mad.

How Lucy Backslid.

I has 'tended some revivals dat was lively in my
    day,
An' I 's seed folks git 'uligion in mos' evah kin'
    o' way;
But I tell you, an' you b'lieve me dat I 's speak-
    in' true indeed,
Dat gal tuk huh 'ligion ha'dah dan de ha'dest
    yit I 's seed.

Well, f'om dat, 't was " Sistah Jackson, won't you
    please do dis er dat? "
She mus' allus sta't de singin' w'en dey 'd pass
    erroun' de hat,
An' hit seemed dey was n't nuffin' in dat chu'ch
    dat could go by
'Dout sistah Lucy Jackson had a finger in de
    pie.

But de sayin' mighty trufeful dat hit easiah to
    sail
W'en de sea is ca'm an' gentle dan to weathah
    out a gale.

Lyrics of the Hearthside.

Dat's whut made dis ooman's trouble; ef de
    sto'm had kep' away,
She 'd 'a' had enough 'uligion fu' to lasted out
    huh day.

Lucy went wid 'Lishy Davis, but w'en she jined
    chu'ch, you know
Dah was lots o' little places dat, of cose, she
    could n't go;
An' she had to gin up dancin' an' huh singin'
    an' huh play. —
Now hit 's nachul dat sich goin's-on 'u'd drive a
    man away.

So, w'en Lucy got so solemn, Ike he sta'ted fu'
    to go
Wid a gal who was a sinnah an' could mek a
    bettah show.
Lucy jes' went on to meetin' lak she did n't keer
    a rap,
But my 'sperunce kep' me t'inkin' dah was
    somep'n' gwine to drap.

222

How Lucy Backslid.

Fu' a gal won't let 'uligion er no othah so't o'
    t'ing
Stop huh w'en she teks a notion dat she wants
    a weddin' ring.
You kin p'omise huh de blessin's of a happy
    aftah life
(An' hit's nice to be a angel), but she 'd ravah
    be a wife.

So w'en Chrismus come an' mastah gin a frolic
    on de lawn,
Did n't 'sprise me not de littlest seein' Lucy
    lookin' on.
An' I seed a wa'nin' lightnin' go a-flashin' f'om
    huh eye
Jest ez 'Lishy an' his new gal went a-gallivantin'
    by.

An' dat Tildy, umph! she giggled, an' she gin
    huh dress a flirt
Lak de people she was passin' was ez common
    ez de dirt;

An' de minit she was dancin', w'y dat gal put
    on mo' aihs
Dan a cat a-tekin' kittens up a paih o' windin'
    staihs.

She could 'fo'd to show huh sma'tness, fu' she
    could n't he'p but know
Dat wid jes' de present dancahs she was ownah
    of de flo';
But I t'ink she'd kin' o' cooled down ef she
    happened on de sly
Fu' to noticed dat 'ere lightnin' dat I seed in
    Lucy's eye.

An' she would n't been so 'stonished w'en de
    people gin a shout,
An' Lucy th'owed huh mantle back an' come
    a-glidin' out.
Some ahms was dah to tek huh an' she fluttahed
    down de flo'
Lak a feddah f'om a bedtick w'en de win' com-
    mence to blow.

How Lucy Backslid.

Soon ez Tildy see de trouble, she jes' tu'n an'
    toss huh haid,
But seem lak she los' huh sperrit, all huh darin'-
    ness was daid.
Did n't cut anothah capah nary time de blessid
    night ;
But de othah one, hit looked lak could n't git
    enough delight.

W'en you keeps a colt a-stan'nin' in de stable
    all along,
W'en he do git out hit 's nachul he 'll be pullin'
    mighty strong.
Ef you will tie up yo' feelin's, hyeah 's de bes'
    advice to tek,
Look out fu' an awful loosin' w'en de string dat
    hol's 'em brek.

Lucy's mammy groaned to see huh, an' huh
    pappy sto'med an' to',
But she kep' right on a-hol'in' to de centah of
    de flo'.

Lyrics of the Hearthside.

So dey went an' ast de pastoh ef he could n't
    mek huh quit,
But de tellin' of de sto'y th'owed de preachah
    in a fit.

Tildy Taylor chewed huh hank'cher twell she'd
    chewed it in a hole, —
All de sinnahs was rejoicin' 'cause a lamb had
    lef' de fol',
An' de las' I seed o' Lucy, she an' 'Lish was
    side an' side :
I don't blame de gal fu' dancin', an' I could n't
    ef I tried.

Fu' de men dat wants to ma'y ain't a-growin'
    'roun' on trees,
An de gal dat wants to git one sholy has to try
    to please.
Hit 's a ha'd t'ing fu' a ooman fu' to pray an' jes'
    set down,
An' to sacafice a husban' so 's to try to gain a
    crown.

How Lucy Backslid.

Now, I don' say she was justified in follerin' huh
    plan ;
But aldough she los' huh 'ligion, yit she sholy
    got de man.
Latah on, w'en she is suttain dat de preachah 's
    made 'em fas'
She kin jes' go back to chu'ch an' ax fu'giveness
    fu' de pas' !